Cairngorms North

Keith Fergus

25 walks
*A comprehensive guidebook to the northern Cairngorms in four areas
Glenmore, Cairn Gorm, Rothiemurchus
& Glen Feshie*

Contents

Introduction

Introduction	4
Using this Guidebook	8

Glenmore — 10

1	Kincardineshire Hills	12
2	Meall a' Bhuachaille	16
3	Creag Mhòr	22
4	Bynack More	28
5	Around Loch Avon	34
6	Stac na h-Iolaire	40

Cairn Gorm — 46

7	Cairn Gorm	48
8	Cairn Gorm & Northern Corries	54
9	Cairn Gorm & Bynack More	60
10	Beinn Mheadhoin	66
11	Ben Macdui	74
12	Ben Macdui via Càrn Etchachan	80
13	Loch Avon Munros	86

Rothiemurchus — 92

14	Braeriach from the Sugarbowl	94
15	Braeriach from Whitewell	100
16	Creag a' Chalamain	106
17	Càrn Eilrig	114
18	Creag Dubh	118
19	Kennapole Hill & Ord Bàn	122
20	Torr Alvie	126

Glen Feshie — 130

21	Sgòr Gaoith	132
22	Monadh Mòr & Beinn Bhrotain	138
23	Mullach Clach a' Bhlàir	146
24	Glen Feshie Munros	150
25	Two Lonely Corbetts	154

Mica Booklist — 160

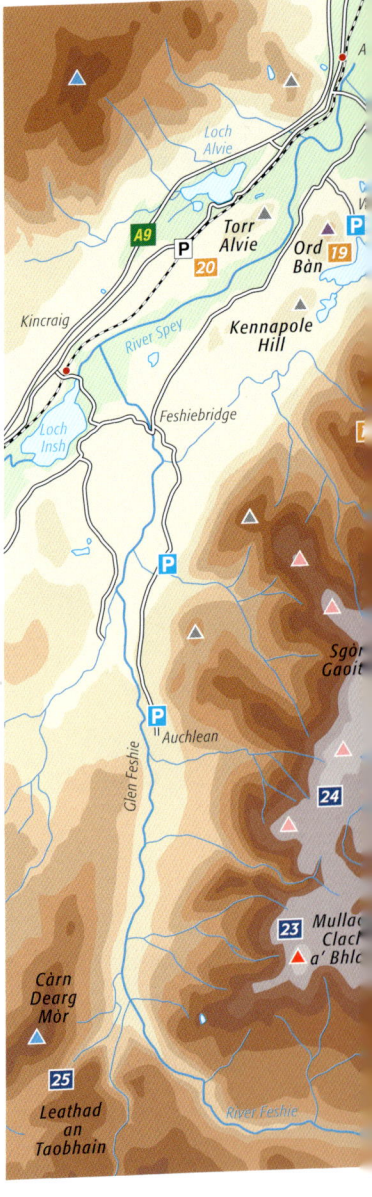

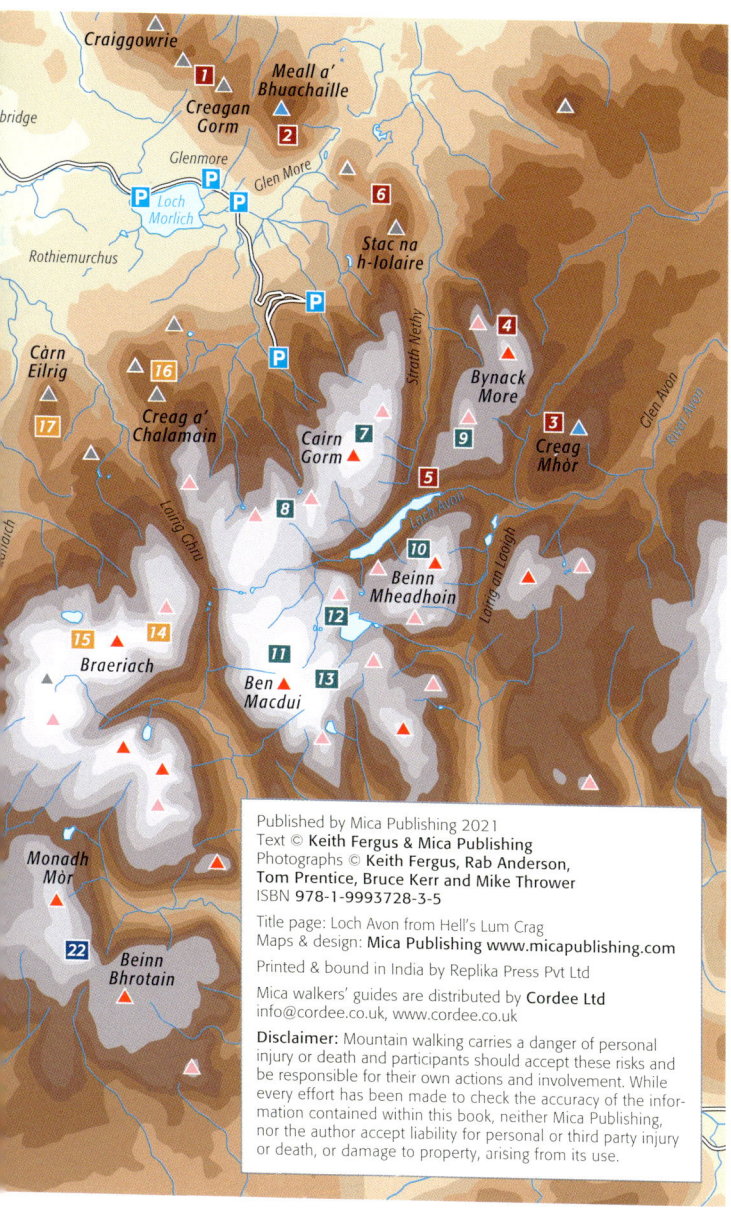

Published by Mica Publishing 2021
Text © **Keith Fergus & Mica Publishing**
Photographs © **Keith Fergus**, Rab Anderson,
Tom Prentice, Bruce Kerr and Mike Thrower
ISBN 978-1-9993728-3-5

Title page: Loch Avon from Hell's Lum Crag
Maps & design: **Mica Publishing** www.micapublishing.com

Printed & bound in India by Replika Press Pvt Ltd

Mica walkers' guides are distributed by **Cordee Ltd**
info@cordee.co.uk, www.cordee.co.uk

Disclaimer: Mountain walking carries a danger of personal injury or death and participants should accept these risks and be responsible for their own actions and involvement. While every effort has been made to check the accuracy of the information contained within this book, neither Mica Publishing, nor the author accept liability for personal or third party injury or death, or damage to property, arising from its use.

Cairngorms North
Introduction

Coire an t-Sneachda from the Fiacaill a' Choire Chais – Cairn Gorm

The Cairngorm mountains are all about size and scale. Comprising the highest and the largest area of arctic-like mountain landscape in Britain, they are the dominant mountain range of the Grampian Mountains in Scotland's North-east Highlands. Covering an area of some 800 square kilometres (500 square miles), the Cairngorms take the form of an area of high plateaux and rounded mountains, within which are five of the six highest mountains in Britain.

Cloaking the lower slopes of these mountains is some of the oldest, finest and most important forest in the world, where rivers and burns course their way through a magnificent landscape. The high peaks, wild moorland, gorgeous woodland and crystal clear streams form a diverse and exceptional landscape that is also a key habitat to a truly astonishing array of wildlife.

The 25 walks in this guidebook lie within the northern Cairngorms area of the main Cairngorm massif, and they all start within a remarkably short drive of the town of Aviemore, which sits on two of the most important lines of transport between the Lowlands and the Highlands of Scotland; the Highland Main Line railway and the A9 road.

The area covered ranges from Meall a' Bhuachaille in the Kincardineshire Hills north of the main Cairngorm massif, to Bynack More and Creag Mhòr which form the eastern edge of the high plateau. Immediately west lies Cairn Gorm itself, the summit after which the massif has been called, from where the Central Plateau extends south to Ben Macdui (Britain's second highest mountain). Continuing westwards lies Braeriach (Britain's third highest mountain), then Sgòr Gaoith and the hills forming the western edge of the high plateau above beautiful Glen Feshie.

As well as taking in all of the major summits in this area, this guidebook

MUNROS: 282 separate mountain summits over 914.4m / 3000ft. Compiled by Sir Hugh Munro in 1891

MUNRO TOPS: 226 subsidiary mountain summits over 914.4m / 3000ft. Compiled by Sir Hugh Munro in 1891

includes a number of minor summits, enabling the walker to venture off the beaten track to visit the wilder corners of this remarkable landscape. Whilst principally a hillwalking guidebook, the mix of routes on high and low mountains and through the dissecting glens and the forests that swath the lower slopes, ensures there is something here for everyone to enjoy and explore in this incredible part of Scotland.

Cairngorms National Park

Ever since the Victorian era, the Cairngorms have been a magnet for outdoor enthusiasts and tourists. Yet it wasn't until 2003 that this spectacular and environmentally important landscape was designated as Scotland's second national park, Loch Lomond and the Trossachs having become the country's first, just one year earlier.

The Cairngorms National Park was established to enhance and conserve the cultural and natural heritage of the area and to nurture the natural resources of the landscape. Other benefits were the development of the social and economic aspects for local communities. It is estimated that 1.4 million people visit the park every year. Covering an area of 4500 square kilometres (1750 sq miles), the Cairngorms National Park is Britain's largest, some 40% bigger than the Lake District and twice the size of Loch Lomond and the Trossachs.

As well as containing five of the six highest mountains in Britain (Ben Macdui, Braeriach, Cairn Toul, Sgòr an Lochain Uaine and Cairn Gorm) within the main Cairngorms area, the greater national park is home to 55 Munros (see panel at top of page) and 26 Corbetts (see panel at top of p7).

Shaping the Landscape

The historic Gaelic name for The Cairngorms is Am Monadh Ruadh, which means The Red Mountains, and relates to the pink or reddish colour of the granite that forms the bedrock for

Allt Mòr and the Kincardineshire Hills

Cairngorms North
Introduction

Cairn Toul, Sgòr an Lochain Uaine and Braeriach from Ben Macdui

the majority of the high Cairngorm summits. However, the name Cairn Gorm itself, which is derived from An Càrn Gorm, means Blue Mountain, and most likely relates to the fact that when seen from a distance the mountain takes on a bluish colour due to the atmosphere filtering out the other colours.

Around 400 million years ago The Cairngorms were part of a huge range that stretched from North America to Norway and were higher than The Alps. This upland table of metamorphic rock was forced high by intense activity deep inside the earth. It was then moulded, through extremes of heat and pressure, over these millions of years, before finally being eroded by ice and water to leave the rounded mountains and vast, granite plateaus we see today.

The Ice Age first began some three million years ago and since then Scotland has been covered by ice sheets and glaciers on a number of occasions. The last great ice sheets covered the whole country including the Cairngorms some 22,000 years ago. Massive glaciers scoured the terrain, creating corries and gouging out great trenches such as the Loch Avon basin, Glen Feshie, Gleann Eanaich, the Làirig Ghru and the Làirig an Laoigh, all of which can be seen and visited using this guide. This period of cooling finally ended some 11,000 years ago and the evidence left behind by the water and debris from the melting ice can also be plainly seen.

Today, from a distance the Cairngorms look like a long, rolling and potentially uninteresting procession of hills. However, for those prepared to look closer, the landscape reveals that they are anything but that. Shapely glens and corries, cliff-lined and boulder-strewn slopes, lochans and waters that are shed from the high plateaux, all combine to make this a truly beautiful and wondrous landscape. This geological marvel has also delivered a critical habitat for flora and fauna.

▲ *CORBETTS: 222 summits between 762m / 2500ft and 914m / 2999ft. Compiled by J Rooke Corbett in the 1930s*

▲ *GRAHAMS: 219 summits between 610m / 2000ft and 761m / 2499ft. Compiled by Alan Dawson & Fiona Graham and named after her*

Natural Highlights

Approximately 16,000 people live within the vast Cairngorms National Park, giving the area a population density of just 4.2 people per square kilometre. What this means is that much of the landscape has seen comparatively little human activity (particularly above 600 metres) leaving plenty of room for wildlife to thrive.

Crucial to the success of the enormous diversity of flora and fauna, is the range of habitats; moorland, bog, woodland, loch, river and mountain plateau, ranging from lower altitudes near the banks of the River Spey, all the way to Ben Macdui at 1309m. Key species such as red deer, pine martin, otter, red squirrel and golden eagle may well be spotted when exploring the woodland and riverbank, or roaming the high plateau.

Yet away from the better known mammals and birdlife is a phenomenal assortment of flora and fauna that prospers within the mixture of habitats; the

Rothiemurchus

rare and endangered capercaillie, osprey, yellow siskin, Scottish crossbill (the only bird unique to the British Isles), crested tit, creeping lady's tresses, harebell and twinflower populate the great remnant of the Caledonian Pine Forest. Brown trout, salmon, grey and pied wagtail and dipper frequent the fast flowing waters of the burns and streams that cascade down towards the River Spey.

It is on the high plateau, however, that a diverse proliferation of wildlife exists. This includes the only free-ranging reindeer herd in Britain, raven, dotterel, skylark, snow bunting, ptarmigan and mountain hare. Insects such as black mountain moth and bilberry bumblebee feed on crowberry and blaeberry while heather, woolly fringe moss, creeping azalea and cladonia lichen form great mattresses beneath your feet.

Wherever you walk within the Cairngorms, a visual and aural treat is guaranteed.

Capercaillie

Cairngorms North
Using this Guidebook

Route Maps & Mapping

Route maps accompanying the walks are drawn from out of copyright Ordnance Survey (OS) mapping, supplemented by in the field GPS tracks and personal observation.

Coloured triangles showing hill and mountain summit locations on maps are as described at the top of pages 5, 7 & 9.

The following symbols are also used on route maps.

Map Symbols
- 🅿 Car park or layby
- 🅿 Other parking

Route Symbols
- ——— Route on path
- ═══ Road
- ━━━ Route along road
- ═ ═ ═ Track
- ▪ ▪ ▪ ▪ Route along track
- - - - - Other path
- ——— Optional extension

These route maps are only sketch maps and walkers are advised to purchase the relevant up-to-date maps, either in paper or digital form, bearing in mind that mobile hand held devices rely on batteries and may lose power.

The Ordnance Survey (OS) is the UK's national mapping authority; *www.ordnancesurvey.co.uk*.

The relevant OS paper maps covering the walks in this guidebook are; Landranger 1:50k scale sheets 35 (Kingussie & Monadhliath Mountains), 36 (Grantown & Aviemore, Cairngorm Mountains) & 43 (Braemar & Blair Atholl) and Explorer 1:25k scale sheet OL 57 (Cairn Gorm & Aviemore).

Scottish-based Harvey maps also produce maps in paper and digital form; *www.harveymaps.co.uk*. The relevant Harvey paper maps are; Cairn Gorm Superwalker (1:25k scale), Cairn Gorm Ultramap (1:40k scale) and Cairngorms British Mountain Map (1:40k scale).

- routes on roads generally follow pavements or verges.

- tracks include all non-tarmac surfaces (farm and forest tracks), and atv (all terrain vehicle) tracks on open hillsides.

- 'pathless' hillsides are often criss-crossed by paths created by sheep, deer, cattle or goats.

Many routes pass through forestry which can be closed to access due to logging or wind-blown trees.

Access

The Land Reform (Scotland) Act 2003 grants everyone the right to be on most land and inland water for recreation, providing they act responsibly. These rights and responsibilities are explained in the Scottish Access Code <www.outdooraccess-scotland.scot>.

- take personal responsibility for your own actions and act safely;

- respect people's privacy and peace of mind;

- help land managers and others to work safely and effectively;

- care for your environment and take your litter home;

- keep your dog under proper control;

- take extra care if you're organising an event or running a business.

▲ **SUB-2000ft MARILYNS:** Marilyns are British Isles wide summits with a prominence of above 150m / 492.1ft. The Sub-2000ft Marilyns fill the 'gap' below the Grahams. The list was created by Alan Dawson and named after Marilyn Monroe as a pun on Munro.

▲ **OTHER Summits:** Other worthwhile summits

Route Times

Time is subjective and influenced by many factors including fitness, terrain, vertical ascent, steepness, and the weather. As such, the timings in this guide are merely indicators of how long a route might take. Timings are for round trips but do NOT include stops for lunch, rests or admiring the view.

Left & Right

In route descriptions, left and right are used looking up on ascent and looking down on descent, unless otherwise stated. In addition, a geographical indicator has often been included to reduce ambiguity.

Equipment & Weather

Sturdy footwear with a good tread is advisable for all walks, as many paths are on natural surfaces of earth or rock and can be wet and slippery.

Scotland's weather can vary significantly from place to place and from hour to hour, even in summer. It is recommended that warm, wind and waterproof clothing be carried, especially above the treeline and on walks that venture onto hill and mountain tops. A torch should also be carried, especially during shorter daylight hours. Adequate food and water should also be taken.

A map and compass and the ability to use them are essential for all walks above the treeline, where an unexpected reduction in visibility may result in serious disorientation. The relatively featureless nature of the high ground in the Cairngorms, together with the severity of the weather it experiences, means that it is a notorious place for navigational errors. GPS units with OS mapping are useful, as are mobile phones, but it should be noted that signal coverage is patchy, especially in the glens. However, both rely on batteries and may lose power.

All of the foregoing is especially relevant in winter. Whilst these mountains are beautiful under cover of snow, this is an arctic-like environment which can be harsh and unforgiving. Wind speeds in excess of 100mph (161 kmh) are common on the summit of Cairn Gorm. As well as being suitably equipped, the winter walker should aquaint themselves with the Scottish Avalanche Information website *www.sais.co.uk* and use this when winter hillwalking.

Weather forecasting is not easy, but the following websites are worthwhile.
www.mwis.org.uk (Mountain Weather Information Service)
www.metoffice.gov.uk
www.bbc.co.uk/weather
BBC tv forecasts can be accessed via terrestrial and satellite services.

Midges & Ticks

Like most upland areas in the UK, Scotland suffers from midges. They are usually worst on warm, damp, overcast days and at dusk, but can be held at bay with various repellents.

Sheep and deer ticks are also prevalent in heather and long grass. Using repellent and wearing trousers tucked into socks will lessen the risk. Ticks can carry Lyme disease and checking for bites after a day's walking is important. For more information visit *www.lymediseaseaction.org.uk*.

Glenmore

1. Kincardineshire Hills 12
2. Meall a' Bhuachaille 16
3. Creag Mhòr 22
4. Bynack More 28
5. Around Loch Avon 34
6. Stac na h-Iolaire 40

Ryvoan Pass and Glen More

1 Kincardineshire Hills
Four summits above Loch Morlich

Craiggowrie, Creag a' Chaillich, Creagan Gorm and Meall a' Bhuachaille

Lying between the Spey Valley and the main Cairngorm massif is the distinctive ridge of the Kincardineshire Hills, formed by Meall a' Bhuachaille, Creagan Gorm, Creag a' Chaillich and Craiggowrie. Meall a' Bhuachaille is the highest point and rising to a height of 810m, it is a Corbett. Although dwarfed by the neighbouring mountains of the Cairngorms, to which they give a grandstand view, these hills offer a short but superb walk.

Begin from the Forestry Commission's car park for its Glenmore Visitor Centre, which is located on the left just beyond the east end of Loch Morlich. There is an interpretation centre, shop, cafe and toilets here.

Above and just behind the Visitor Centre, follow a path into the trees signposted for Meall a' Bhuachaille.

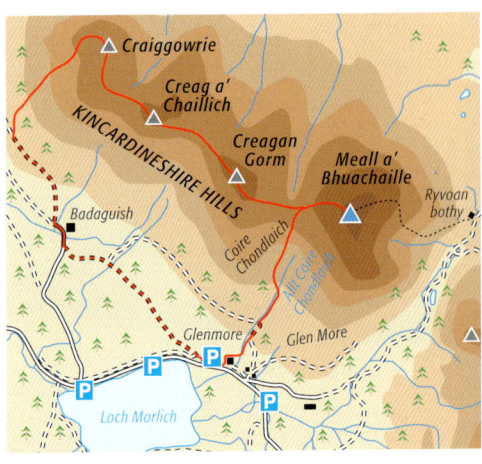

START & FINISH: Glenmore Visitor Centre Car Park (NN976098); pay & display
DISTANCE: 13km; 8 miles
HEIGHT GAIN: 700m; 2297ft
APPROX TIME: 4–5hrs

Part of the Glenmore Forest Park, this is The Queen's Forest (named for Queen Mary during the 1935 Silver Jubilee of King George V) and it is dominated by birch and Scots pine. Gain a track and turn left along this with the Allt Coire Chondlaich to your left. When the track ends, continue in the same direction to emerge onto the open hillside beneath Coire Chondlaich where the path swings right to ascend the steeper hillside, with marvellous views behind to the main Cairngorm massif.

Like many paths within the National Park, this one has been expertly constructed, and it is a relatively simple pull over heathery ground to reach a point just above the col at 624m between Creagan Gorm and Meall a' Bhuachaille to its right.

Turn right and ascend the path that winds quite steeply east to reach the broad summit of Meall a' Bhuachaille (810m); Hill of the Herdsman. It is a grand viewpoint and a good spot for a break beside its large cairn and wind shelter. A shorter route, Meall a' Bhuachaille [2], climbs to here from the east side of the hill, reached via the Ryvoan Pass. On a clear day the bulk of

Loch Morlich from Meall a' Bhuachaille

Kincardineshire Hills

Meall a' Bhuachaille from Creagan Gorm

Ben Wyvis and the softer margins of the Moray coastline are visible to the north, although it is the immediate view south that really strikes a chord – Bynack More [4], Cairn Gorm [7] and its Northern Corries, then Braeriach [14].

Retrace your steps towards the col, then take a path off right and drop to the marshy low point; keep an eye out for the roaming reindeer herd here. A steady ascent north-west of just over 100m in height gains the summit of Creagan Gorm (732m); Little Rocky Blue Hill. Again the panorama is extensive, taking in the lower reaches of the National Park, including Loch Morlich and the vast wooded landscape of Rothiemurchus.

The high-level ridge then undulates across this quiet landscape in the company of skylark, meadow pipit and wheatear, crossing more boggy ground in the dips and passing a large granite boulder dumped by the Ice Age to reach double-topped Creag a' Chaillich (711m); Crag of the Old Woman or Witch. A last push north reaches Craiggowrie (687m); Crag of the Goat. The final summit of the day, it is another wonderful vantage point. A stone wind shelter just beyond the top allows one to sit and take in the view that now extends up and down the Spey Valley.

After a brief, steep drop, the path swings left over a slight rise, then descends gradually, returning to the

Creag a' Chaillich

Kincardineshire Hills

Cairn Gorm from the track to Glenmore

Queen's Forest. The path is eroded and boggy in places but once within the woodland it improves. Continue downhill, keeping left to reach a track, then turn left along this to walk through the forest, emerging to a more open area with views to the main Cairngorm massif.

Turn left onto a road and follow this through Badaguish Outdoor Centre with its log cabins and chalets. On the far side, where the road sweeps right, go left along a track past a barrier. Follow this track east through a cleared area with views up to Creagan Gorm on the ridge then take the right fork south-east back into the forest.

As you descend, Loch Morlich comes into view through the trees and at a cleared area there are pleasing views across to Cairn Gorm, the Northern Corries, Braeriach and Càrn Eilrig [17]. On reaching the main road, turn left and follow a minor road up behind Glenmore Youth Hostel to return to the top end of the Visitor Centre car park.

Skylark

One of the most widespread of upland birds, the skylark is seen to lower levels on open ground on almost every walk in the Cairngorms. Slightly bigger than a sparrow, it is a nervy, brown-streaked bird with a crested head. Initially difficult to spot, it is instantly recognisable due to the male birds singing; a fast, continual outpour of long-lasting rolling chirruping and whistling. Birds can then be detected high above, hovering with rapid wing flaps and more readily seen as they glide to ground in song to suddenly fold their wings and fall silent as they land.

Meall a' Bhuachaille
Hill of the Herdsman

Meall a' Bhuachaille from Glen More

Meall a' Bhuachaille is the highest point of the Kincardineshire Hills, which rise above Loch Morlich, to the north of the main Cairngorm massif. This short but scenic route heads through Glenmore to beautiful An Lochan Uaine, then through Ryvoan Pass to Ryvoan bothy. From there, a good path leads to the summit, then descends into the Glenmore Forest Park on the return.

A convenient start can be made from the Glenmore Visitor Centre, which has an interpretation centre, shop, cafe and toilets. Walk past the centre, go around a barrier, cross a side road and pass the Cairngorm Reindeer Centre (see p83) onto a single-track road. Follow this for 100m then bear left onto a shared use footpath and cycleway. This progresses easily above the road for 1km to join a track on the other side of a barrier at the road end just beyond Glenmore Lodge; Scotland's National Outdoor Training Centre.

Turn left, signposted Forest Lodge and Nethy Bridge, and walk north-east along the track. This is the Rathad nam Meirleach (Road of the Thieves), which was used by groups of Highlanders

START & FINISH: Glenmore Visitor Centre Car Park (NN 976098); pay & display
DISTANCE: 9.5km; 6 miles
HEIGHT GAIN: 480m; 1575ft
APPROX TIME: 3–4hrs

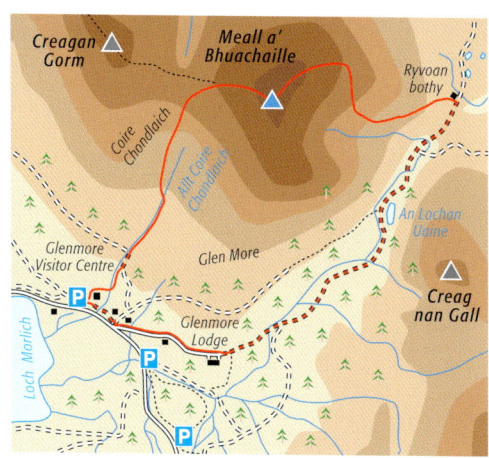

drive their great herds of cattle south from the Highlands along the Làirig an Laoigh (Pass of the Calves) and onwards to the great livestock markets, or trysts, at Falkirk, Perth, the Scottish Borders and Northern England. The track runs through the beautiful surrounds of Glen More; a remnant of the Caledonian Forest where birds such as crested tit and Scottish crossbill may well be spotted, together with mammals such as red squirrel and pine marten.

between the 14th and 17th centuries, who supplemented their income by stealing cattle from glens to the south and steering them back to their upland areas. In later years, drovers would

With the wooded lower slopes of Meall a' Bhuachaille rising steeply to the north, carry on for 1.5km to An

Meall a' Bhuachaille's lower slopes

17

Meall a' Bhuachaille

An Lochan Uaine and the Ryvoan Pass

Lochan Uaine. This stunning little loch is notable for the vibrant emerald colour of its water; the translation from the Gaelic is The Little Green Loch. It is said that the colour originates from the legendary Glen More fairies that used to wash their green garments in the loch. A more likely explanation however, is rock minerals beneath the surface. Either drop down steps to the loch, or take a path on the right to a small viewing platform and enjoy the spectacle along its length.

After leaving the confines of An Lochan Uaine, cross the flat valley floor and continue through the narrow defile of the Ryvoan Pass, hemmed in by the slopes of Meall a' Bhuachaille and Creag nan Gall. Soon the track splits at the exit from the pass, with right being the way to Strath Nethy and the Làirig an Laoigh, as followed by **Creag Mhòr** [3] and **Bynack More** [4].

Keep left though and make the gradual ascent to arrive at the small but perfectly formed Ryvoan bothy, which is

Meall a' Bhuachaille

I Leave Tonight From Euston

I shall leave tonight from Euston
By the seven-thirty train,
And from Perth in the early morning
I shall see the hills again.
From the top of Ben Macdhui
I shall watch the gathering storm,
And see the crisp snow lying
At the back of Cairngorm.
I shall feel the mist from Bhrotain
and the pass by Larig Ghru
To look on dark Loch Einich
From the heights of Sgoran Dubh.
From the broken Barns of Bynack
I shall see the sunrise gleam
On the forehead of Ben Rinnes
And Strathspey awake from dream.
And again in the dusk of evening
I shall find once more alone
The dark water of the Green Loch,
And the pass beyond Ryvoan.
For tonight I leave from Euston
And leave the world behind;
Who has the hills as a lover,
Will find them wondrous kind.

A.M. Lawrence

beautifully situated overlooking the Abernethy Forest on the edge of the Cairngorm massif. Up until the late 19th century it formed part of a farmhouse, but today Ryvoan is just one of around 100 similar shelters across Britain maintained by the Mountain Bothies Association. A tradition states that a poem, I Leave Tonight from Euston, written by A.M.Lawrence in the 1950s, is kept on the door at Ryvoan. Lawrence spent much of her childhood at nearby Nethy Bridge.

Meall a' Bhuachaille

Meall a' Bhuachaille from Ryvoan bothy

The route now strikes west up the heather-clad eastern flanks of Meall a' Bhuachaille. It's a steep ascent but a well-engineered path makes the going a lot easier. After an initial long, rising traverse to the south-west, the path swings right up a steeper section with stone steps; if a break is required the expanding vista and the view back down to teardrop-shaped An Lochan Uaine give worthy excuses. In a while the incline eases and a final gradual ascent to the south-west gains Meall a' Bhuachaille's 810m summit and large shelter cairn.

It is a marvellous vantage point. Ben Rinnes stands out to the north-east and, on a clear day, the prominent cone of Morven can be seen some 70 miles (112km) distant to the north across the Moray Firth. However, it is the view of the main Northern Cairngorm massif to the south that really catches the eye, particularly the great whaleback of Bynack More to the left with Cairn Gorm itself and the ragged outline of the Northern Corries to the right.

Crested Tit
Closely associated with the Cairngorms, this wonderful bird spends almost all its life in the native Scots pine forests, with its nests being built in dead or decaying trees. It has a distinctive black and white head and short spiky crest and is nearly always on the move for food, feeding mainly on moths, caterpillars and beetles. With only 1000-2000 pairs remaining in Scotland, it has a specially protected status

Meall a' Bhuachaille

Bynack More from Meall a' Bhuachaille

To descend, head to the west. Initially the path is a little vague but soon becomes clear as it drops steadily towards the col between Meall a' Bhuachaille and Creagan Gorm. The route over the Kincardine Hills [1] continues up Creagan Gorm from the col. However, this shorter route bears left on the main path just above the lowest point, leaving the ridge behind to descend south-west into Coire Chondlaich, with a fine view of Loch Morlich and the Rothiemurchus Forest. The path soon swings left, then continues down by the Allt Coire Chondlaich into Glenmore Forest Park to join a track.

Where this track turns left, watch for a signed path on the right, then follow this path down by the burn through attractive Scots pine and birch woodland to regain the car park.

Cairn Gorm from Coire Chondlaich

3
Creag Mhòr
A remote Corbett & secluded mountain refuge

Bynack More from the summit of Creag Mhòr

Located to the east of Bynack More in the Abernethy National Nature Reserve, Creag Mhòr is a remote and unassuming Corbett that sits above the through route to the Làirig an Laoigh pass, which lies to the south. It is a mountain that doesn't receive much footfall, particularly when compared to its bigger neighbour Bynack More, which well and truly overshadows it.

However, this lower height and its location deep in this part of the Cairngorms does mean that its summit is a fine viewpoint from which to survey the grandeur of the surroundings, making it well worth the energy required to get there. Reaching Creag Mhòr and the Fords of Avon Refuge, which lies just beyond it, is made somewhat easier by following the traditional drovers' route to the Làirig an Laoigh, the lesser-known of the two major passes through the Cairngorms, which links Speyside with Deeside (see p36).

The walk starts from the Glenmore Visitor Centre car park at the eastern end of Loch Morlich. The centre has a shop, cafe, toilets and an interpretation centre detailing the history, flora and fauna of the local area.

Head east through the car park and, once around a barrier, cross a side road then pass the Cairngorm Reindeer Centre, which tells the story of, and offers tours to visit, the only free-ranging herd in Britain (see p83). At a single-track road go left, then after 100m bear left onto a shared use cycle route and footpath, which travels easily alongside the road for 1km to just

START & FINISH: Glenmore Visitor Centre Car Park (NN976098); pay & display
DISTANCE: 30.5km; 19 miles
HEIGHT GAIN: 940m; 3084ft
APPROX TIME: 8hrs 30mins–9hrs 30mins

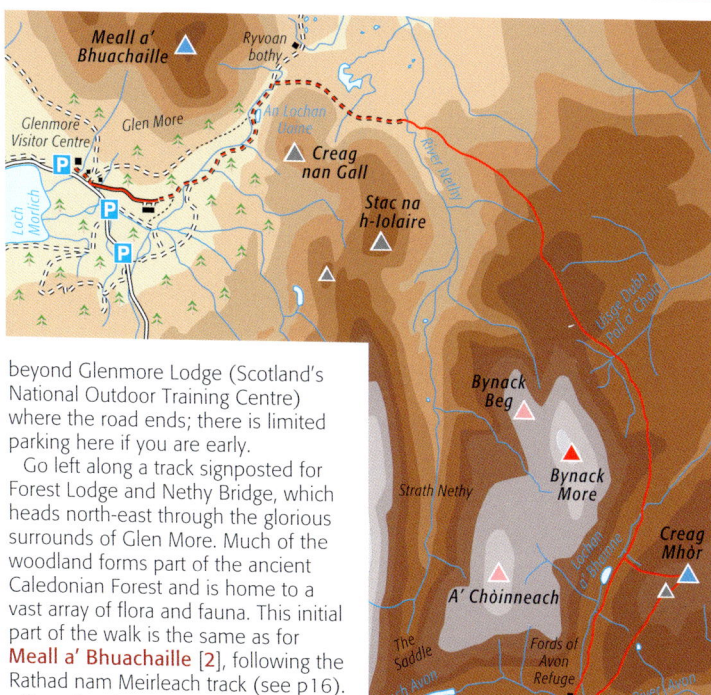

beyond Glenmore Lodge (Scotland's National Outdoor Training Centre) where the road ends; there is limited parking here if you are early.

Go left along a track signposted for Forest Lodge and Nethy Bridge, which heads north-east through the glorious surrounds of Glen More. Much of the woodland forms part of the ancient Caledonian Forest and is home to a vast array of flora and fauna. This initial part of the walk is the same as for **Meall a' Bhuachaille** [2], following the Rathad nam Meirleach track (see p16).

Soon the slopes steepen on either side as you head through the narrow gap between Meall a' Bhuachaille and Creag nan Gall, passing lovely An Lochan Uaine (The Little Green Loch). This is the Ryvoan Pass, and at its far end where the track forks, left to Ryvoan bothy and right to Braemar via the old drove road, take the right-hand stony track.

The track climbs gradually south-east into the Abernethy National Nature Reserve (see p28), another vast tract of moorland and woodland, before dropping to cross a footbridge over the River Nethy; it is possible to mountain bike to here for anyone wishing to shorten the walking distance. Ahead, the path can be seen climbing steadily to the north of Bynack More's huge bulk.

Although it is a prolonged climb, a superbly constructed path makes the going relatively simple and there are great views into Strath Nethy. After 3km the path splits on a broad expanse of wild, featureless ridge where the vegetation has been cut low by the wind. In poor visibility it could become confusing here.

Bynack More [4] takes the right-hand

Creag Mhòr

Wind-scoured terrain on the approach to the summit of Creag Mhòr

path, but the route to Creag Mhòr lies along the left-hand path, which veers south-east off the line of the ridge to reach the highest point of the drove route to the Làirig an Laoigh at just under 800m. Bynack More towers above and the path drops into the secluded landscape of Coire Odhar. The granite-studded top of Creag Mhòr is now in view ahead with Bheinn a' Bhuird and Ben Avon beyond.

Cross the Uisge Dubh Poll a' Choin, which is normally straightforward; there are stepping stones a few metres upstream, although there could be a problem if the water was running high. After a muddy section, the path improves and rises gradually over a crest where Creag Mhòr's long ridgeline really comes into view. There are some further wetter sections as the path drops into the Corrie of the Barns at the start of the through route to the Làirig an Laoigh proper. Cross the Glasath burn, and again, although there are stepping stones there could be problems if the water was high. Now some distance from any road, there is a real remote feel to the walk.

Continue on the path for 300m or so, then break off left to ascend the pathless north-western slopes of Creag Mhòr. Fortunately it is only a climb of about 200m, initially over some steep and quite wet ground, before a more gradual and drier rise gains the summit, which lies to the left and is adorned by a granite tor (895m) with some fine examples of wind and water-created

Creag Mhòr

potholes in the solid granite. The view extends along Glen Avon and the sinuous course of the River Avon while Bynack More and its Barns, Beinn a' Bhuird, Beinn a' Chaorainn, Beinn Mheadhoin and Cairn Gorm number amongst the mountains on show.

The pathless, rough terrain continues and in poor visibility the descent could be tricky. However, on a clear day the route down to the Fords of Avon Refuge is relatively straightforward, crossing first to the lower South West top (875m), then dropping south-west on a steady incline across heathery, bouldery ground to join the path again.

Cross the clear, fast-flowing waters of the Allt Dearg, by stepping stones and continue for 200m to reach the Fords of Avon Refuge. Located beside the River Avon and set amongst some spectacular mountain scenery, this remote shelter is an ideal spot for a break. A basic one small room small hut, it can sleep up to four people, although it is very much seen as an emergency shelter.

The refuge was built in 1970 and

then rebuilt in August 2011 by the Mountain Bothies Association (MBA), the RSPB and Glenmore Lodge. Today it is cared for by the MBA. **Around Loch Avon** [5] travels upstream from here to the Loch Avon basin.

To return, follow the path northwards under the steep slopes of A' Chòinnich and Creag Mhòr, soon passing little Lochan a' Bhainne, back to the Glasath burn. It is then a matter of retracing your steps over the untamed landscape back to Glen More and the start.

Creag Mhòr across the head of Corrie of the Barns from Bynack More

Across Loch Morlich to Rothiemurchus, Càrn Eilrig and Creag Dhubh

4 Bynack More
Great granite-studded whaleback

Stac na h-Iolaire &
Meall a' Bhuachaille from Bynack More

Rising to a height of 1090m at the eastern end of the Northern Cairngorm massif, Bynack More is a big, bulky Munro that sits above the Abernethy National Nature Reserve. It provides a superb vantage point from which to view the Reserve and much of the National Park. Excellent tracks and paths lead to the summit, but beyond this the terrain is rougher and mostly pathless as the route crosses A' Chòinneach before dropping to beautiful Loch Avon with its dramatic mountain backdrop. The return is via Strath Nethy, through whose remote confines, runs a rough and at times muddy path.

Start from the Allt Mòr car park, which

Abernethy National Nature Reserve
This important reserve encompasses moorland, bog, woodland and mountain plateau, from Garten Wood, near the banks of the River Spey, all the way to Ben Macdui, the second highest mountain in Britain. Abernethy means 'Mouth of the Bright or Shining River' and relates to the River Nethy that spills from the high Cairngorm mountains through Strath Nethy.

Bynack More also sits within the reserve, which covers a huge 130sq km (50sq miles), and holds the largest surviving remnant of ancient Caledonian pinewood. Abernethy also has one of the few areas of fragile bog moorland left in Britain. Here stunted pine trees (some over 350 years old) grow sparingly over the bog surface and provide a valuable habitat for invertebrates. There is a good path network running through the reserve, where a number of habitats can be easily explored and an extensive array of flora and fauna seen; osprey, yellow siskin, Scottish crossbill, capercaillie and large pinewood grouse are just a few species. In fact an incredible 4500 variety of plants and animals (800 of which are nationally scarce or rare) have been recorded within the reserve.

START & FINISH: Allt Mòr Car Park (NH983088); pay & display
DISTANCE: 29km; 18 miles
HEIGHT GAIN: 860m; 2822ft
APPROX TIME: 8hrs 30mins–9hrs 30mins

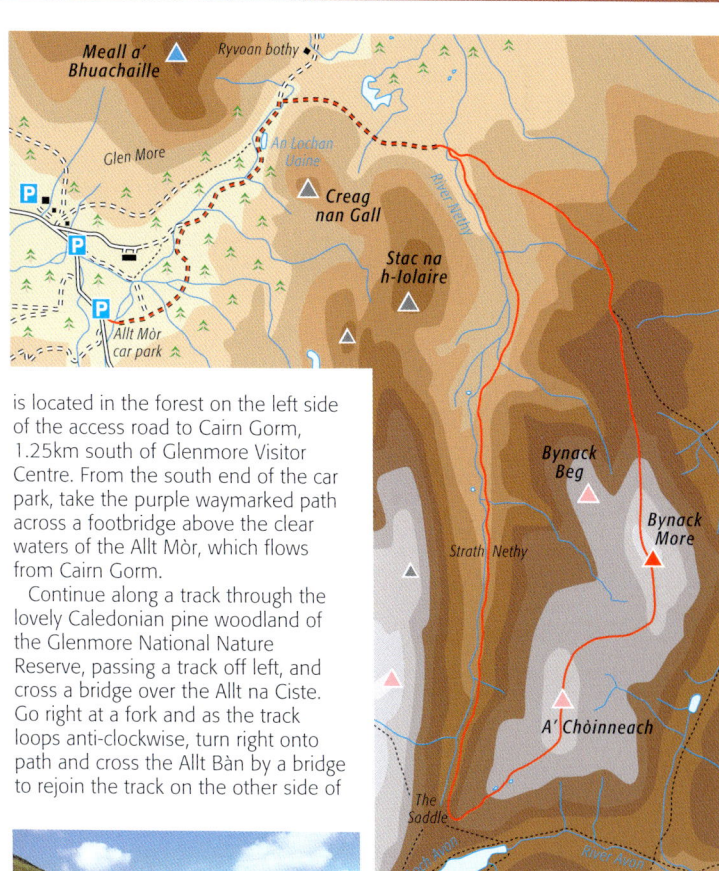

is located in the forest on the left side of the access road to Cairn Gorm, 1.25km south of Glenmore Visitor Centre. From the south end of the car park, take the purple waymarked path across a footbridge above the clear waters of the Allt Mòr, which flows from Cairn Gorm.

Continue along a track through the lovely Caledonian pine woodland of the Glenmore National Nature Reserve, passing a track off left, and cross a bridge over the Allt na Ciste. Go right at a fork and as the track loops anti-clockwise, turn right onto path and cross the Allt Bàn by a bridge to rejoin the track on the other side of

River Nethy & Meall a' Bhuachaille

a ford. Continue to meet the main track from the road end at Glenmore Lodge and turn right along this; the Rathad nam Meirleach, Road of the Thieves (see p16).

Now on the track that travels north-east through Glenmore Forest along the

Bynack More

Bynack More and Bynack Beg

floor of the glen, continue past An Lochan Uaine (The Little Green Loch) then through the Ryvoan Pass, which is hemmed in by the steep slopes of Meall a' Bhuachaille and Creag nan Gall. Where the pass starts to open out, take the right-hand fork in the track (signposted for Braemar), which is the route of the old drove road between Speyside and Deeside (see p36).

Now traversing the base of the hills, the track runs through the Abernethy National Nature Reserve past Loch a' Gharbh-choire, with fine views extending north across a wonderful open landscape. Creag nan Gall & **Stac na h-Iolaire** [6] lie to the right separated by the Eag Gharbh-choire glacial meltwater channel.

The track ends just before a footbridge across the River Nethy, at the mouth of Strath Nethy where there is a wonderful view of Bynack More's granite-studded top. It can be mountain biked to here for anyone wishing to shorten the walking distance. Cross the

Bynack More summit - distant Ben Rinnes

Bynack More

Little Barns of Bynack More

bridge and follow the superbly constructed path which ascends south-east up the broad shoulder of Bynack More. As height is gained the sense of space is palpable and if a breather is required then the outlook along Strath Nethy, to the steep eastern slopes of Cairn Gorm, or north all the way to the sinuous profile of Ben Rinnes, is worth stopping for.

Where the path splits after 3km on the broad shoulder, take the right-hand path which heads south towards the great whaleback ridge leading to the towering summit of Bynack More, with Bynack Beg to its right. The left-hand path leads to **Creag Mhòr** [3] and the Làirig an Laoigh and is also followed by **Around Loch Avon** [5].

After a gentle climb across a broad plateau, the final ascent begins. Steeper sections are aided by the path zigzagging up Bynack More's north ridge and it is not long before the granite-topped summit crest is reached and a vista of exceptional proportions. Ben Avon, Beinn a' Bhuird, Beinn Mheadhoin, Ben Macdui and Cairn Gorm are some of the big Cairngorm mountains vying for attention, while to the north the flatter plains of Moray draw the eye all the way to its coastline and, on a clear day, beyond to conical Morven and the mountains of Caithness in the far north. The summit lies towards the south end.

If the subsidiary Munro Top (see p5) of Bynack Beg (970m) is to be ascended, then it is best to leave the ascent path up Bynack More at its foot, just below a prominent outcrop. From there, a rough path slants up right across the slope to the col at the head of Coire Dubh, from where the top lies a short distance to the north-west. It is

Barns of Bynack More

Bynack More

a good spot to appreciate the size of Bynack More, as well as the steeper slopes dropping into Strath Nethy. A path is then followed uphill to gain the crest of Bynack More a short distance from its summit. This adds about 15mins to the day.

The alternative is to continue up the ridge to Bynack More, then descend to pick up Bynack Beg, from where a traverse south can be made to the col with A' Chòinneach. This will most likely mean missing out on the Little Barns and Barns of Bynack, unless a reascent to the ridge is made.

From the summit of Bynack More, head south down the gentle ridge to reach the fine granite tors of the Little Barns of Bynack. The much larger and more impressive Barns of Bynack stand a little to the east, some 50m lower down, and are worth a visit.

Leaving the Bynack More ridgeline, walk downhill to the south-west onto a flat, wind-scoured plateau, which at 940m is higher than many Munros. As a result it should be given the corresponding respect, particularly in poor weather. Underfoot can be a little marshy but this provides an ideal habitat for flora, including woolly fringe moss and creeping azalea.

Continue south-west and gradually rise over spongy, mossy slopes to swing south onto A' Chòinneach (1016m), another subsidiary Munro Top, whose summit is marked with a small cairn. Keep on south, enjoying a stunning view of the mountains around the Loch Avon basin; Beinn Mheadhoin, Càrn Etchachan, Ben Macdui and Cairn Gorm. As the ground begins to fall gradually south-west, a fantastic view of Loch Avon is the reward. Continue down the ridge past some small lochans on a path that drops towards the loch.

Eventually, just above Loch Avon, an intersection of paths is gained at The Saddle. Make a right turn here and walk north into the deep defile of Strath Nethy and descend beneath the

Bynack More and the Little Barns from the A' Chòinneach col

Bynack More

Loch Avon and Ben Macdui from A' Chòinneach

boulder fields falling from high on Cnap Coire na Spreidhe to the left. Initially the path is clear but becomes fainter and rougher as it heads along the east bank of the Garbh Allt, which soon becomes the River Nethy. It is a challenging section of the walk, with the glen hemmed in on both sides by steep slopes, giving it a remote and lonely air.

However, once across the Allt a' Choire Dearg, which descends from Bynack More, the landscape begins to open out and the path improves a little, although there are times it can be very wet. Keeping to the right side, the path sticks close to the River Nethy, eventually reaching the bridge over it where the outward route is followed back through the Ryvoan Pass.

Crossbill
All three species of crossbill are found in the Cairngorms (Scottish crossbill, common crossbill and parrot crossbill), however the Scottish crossbill (loxia Scotica) is a distinct species and it is the only bird unique to the British Isles. The Crossbill's diet consists chiefly of seeds from Scots pines and its preferred habitat is the Caledonian pine forest. As a result, this lovely little bird is found principally in the North-east Highlands, where the remnants of this ancient woodland exist on any great scale. They use their unusual beak shape to extract the seeds from the cone. Both sexes have browny grey wings and tail, but the male has russet or red plumage, whilst the female has green or yellow plumage.

5 Around Loch Avon
A circuit of one of Scotland's finest lochs

South-west along Loch Avon

Although this fabulous walk twice attains a height of around 800m, it does not venture onto the high-level Cairngorm plateau. Penetrating deep into the heart of the Cairngorm massif by a relatively low-level route, it utilises a landscape shaped by glaciation to reach the River Avon and follows this to its source in the Loch Avon Basin.

Here, amidst magnificent scenery, the route goes around beautiful Loch Avon before returning via The Saddle and another of the National Park's remotest corners, Strath Nethy. A long day, it can also be undertaken as a more leisurely two day trip with an overnight stay camping at either the Fords of Avon Refuge (see p25) or by the side of Loch Avon.

The Glenmore Visitor Centre car park, at the eastern end of Loch Morlich, is one possible start point; The routes over the Kincardineshire Hills [1] and Meall a' Bhuachaille [2] also begin here. Walk east past the Cairngorm Reindeer Centre to gain the access road to Glenmore Lodge (Scotland's National Outdoor Training Centre) and take the shared use footpath and cycleway beside it to reach the road

START & FINISH: Glenmore Visitor Centre Car Park (NN976098); pay & display
DISTANCE: 34.5km; 21.5 miles
HEIGHT GAIN: 700m; 2297ft
APPROX TIME: 9–10hrs

end at The Lodge; there is limited parking here if you arrive early.

Continue ahead on the track of the Thieves' Road (see p16), signposted for Forest Lodge and Nethy Bridge, and walk north-east through beautiful Glen More with its native Caledonian pine trees, which cloak much of the landscape here and play a key role in the biodiversity of the area. After 400m a track joins from the right, from the Allt Mòr car park used for **Bynack More** [4], which also comes this way; the distance to here is the same as from the Visitor Centre, so it too could be used as a start point. Keep on past lovely An Lochan Uaine (The Little Green Loch), then through the narrow Ryvoan Pass, hemmed in by the steep slopes of Meall a' Bhuachaille and Creag nan Gall.

When the track splits, bear right on the route to Braemar by the Làirig an

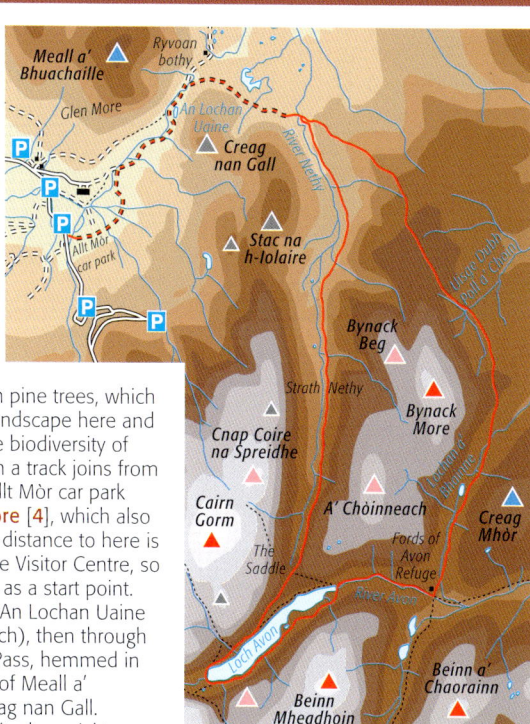

Laoigh. After the confines of the glen, the route now heads along the foot of the hills overlooking the open landscape of the Abernethy National Nature Reserve (see p28). The track ends at a footbridge across the River Nethy after 5.5km; it can be mountain biked to here. On the other side, the route continues as a superbly constructed path, rising steadily above Strath Nethy towards shapely Bynack More.

When the path forks on the broad, flat ridge in a further 3km, take the left branch away from the path leading to

Around Loch Avon

Bynack More from the Uisge Dubh Poll a' Choin in Coire Odhar

the upper whalebacked ridge of Bynack More and continue along a gentle rise to the highpoint at 790m. There is a real sense of space as the path crosses this wind-scoured expanse of wild terrain; ptarmigan, raven and snow bunting may well be spotted hereabouts. On a clear day route finding is simple but at points the path can become a little vague and in poor visibility it could be confusing.

Descend south-east into Coire Odhar and cross the Uisge Dubh Poll a' Choin burn. This can cause problems when running high and even when the water levels are low your feet may get wet; although a few metres upstream stepping stones can make the crossing easier. A muddy path begins to climb, soon rising over a crest, with some

> ### Làirig an Laoigh & the River Avon
> *Cutting through the eastern side of the Cairngorm massif, the Làirig an Laoigh pass links Speyside with Deeside. It means the Pass of the Calves but it is also known locally as An Làirig Shios, The Eastern Pass, whilst the better known Làirig Ghru is called An Làirig Shuas, The Western Pass. Historically the Làirig an Laoigh was used as a drove route, where cattle were taken through the Cairngorms to markets in the south. From the entrance to Strath Nethy, cattle were driven over the north ridge of Bynack More into the làirig. As the route was lower than that through the Làirig Ghru, and not as rough underfoot, it was easier for younger cattle to contend with, hence its name as pass of the calves. At its peak, during the 17th and 18th centuries, thousands of cattle were driven this way each year. Although not as grand as the Làirig Ghru, the Làirig an Laoigh route climbs higher than many Scottish mountains and travels through a superb landscape. These passes now provide convenient access routes enabling the walker to penetrate deep into the Cairngorm massif with relative ease.*
> *The Làirig an Laoigh route crosses the River Avon, which rises from the wild beauty of Loch Avon and flows through lonely Glen Avon to Tomintoul some 35km to the north-east. After a further 25km or so through Strath Avon it finally joins with the River Spey, which then empties into the North Sea at Spey Bay.*

Around Loch Avon

further wetter sections as the path drops into the Corrie of the Barns where the Glasath burn is crossed. There are stepping stones, but again this could be problematic in spate.

Continue uphill on the path, now in the glacial channel that runs all the way through to Deeside, bounded by the steep slopes of Creag Mhòr [3] and Bynack More [4]. Far removed from any road or settlements, there is a real sense of isolation. Lochan a' Bhainne soon comes into view and beyond this a gradual descent leads beneath the steep slopes of Leachd a' Bhainne and the Allt Dearg waterfall.

Approaching Glen Avon, Dubh Lochan can be seen on the far side nestling in the Làirig an Laoigh beneath the steep flanks of Beinn a' Chaorainn and Beinn Mheadhoin. Cross the Allt Dearg by stepping stones then continue for another 200m to reach the Fords of Avon Refuge (see p25).

Loch Avon and Stac an Fhàraidh

With Cairn Gorm in view, now follow the path upstream beside the River Avon for just over 1.5km to reach Loch Avon. Sitting in the base of a deep U-shaped valley at an altitude of 730m and surrounded by cliffs, it is a truly beautiful loch set amongst some of the finest mountain scenery in the country. Left behind by the Ice Age when a huge glacier carved a deep, linear basin, it is known as a ribbon lake, similar to Loch Eanaich in the Gleann

Hell's Lum Crag and Stag Rocks at the head of the Loch Avon basin

Around Loch Avon

Stacan Dubha from the shallows at the head of Loch Avon

Eanaich glacial trough, west of Braeriach.

The walk can be shortened here by bearing right onto a path that climbs to The Saddle between Cairn Gorm and A'Chòinneach at the head of Strath Nethy. However, this misses out the best part, which is to make a delightful circuit of this most scenic of lochs and its magnificent surroundings. Whilst it looks like a fair way, it only takes about 1hr 30mins to walk around to reach The Saddle — excluding time spent stopping to soak up the atmosphere.

Cross the outflow by stepping stones if the water is low, or by a refreshing

Càrn Etchachan and Shelter Stone Crag from the north side of Loch Avon

Around Loch Avon

Strath Nethy

paddle across the shallows. On the other side, a rough path leads easily up the south side of Loch Avon, passing beneath the cliffs of Creag Dhubh and Stacan Dubha, to reach the head of the loch where Càrn Etchachan and the great stone bastion of the Shelter Stone crag dominate. This is a truly wondrous and captivating place, a great amphitheatre surrounded by cliffs, with cascading burns and waterfalls tumbling into it.

The easiest crossing is at the inflow, either by stepping stones, or a paddle across the granitic sands. Follow the lochside path (not the one that slants up to Coire Raibeirt as used by the Beinn Mheadhoin [10] route) back down the other side, being mindful of the gaps between the boulders. When the path forks beneath the cliffs of Stac an Fhàraidh, go left and ascend to The Saddle, at 807m the highest point of the route.

Take the path that heads north into the narrow margins of Strath Nethy. Bounded by steep slopes and passing beneath the impressive boulder fields that fall from high on Cnap Coire na Spreidhe to the left, the path runs beside the Garbh Allt, which drops through the higher part of the glen. The Garbh Allt becomes the River Nethy with the path getting fainter and rougher, and some sections can be wet, which makes this the most challenging section of the walk.

After crossing the Allt a' Choire Dearg the landscape softens a little as the strath starts to open. Eventually the footbridge over the River Nethy is reached, from where it's a simple return through Glen More to the start.

6 Stac na h-Iolaire
Back to the Ice Age

Cairn Gorm from Creag nan Gall

Although sitting prominently between Meall a' Bhuachaille and Cairn Gorm, Creag nan Gall (622m) and Stac na h-Iolaire (742m) are to all extents completely overshadowed and seldom given a second look. Therein lies their attraction though, for this relatively short walk takes you into rarely visited terrain, which offers a different perspective of the surrounding mountains, as well exploring some interesting glacial landform features. A word of caution, despite the low height, the rough terrain and lack of good paths makes this walk more difficult that most on the higher tops!

A start is made from the small Allt Bàn car park, which is located on the left side of the access road to Cairn Gorm, immediately before the bridge over the Abhainn Ruigh-eunachan, 0.5km beyond Glenmore Visitor Centre. There are also roadside parking bays.

Head upstream beside the river, following a track into the lovely Caledonian pine woodland of the Glenmore National Nature Reserve. After 700m or so, cross a footbridge over the river and continue for 300m to meet a track coming from the Allt Mòr car park on the right, which can also be used as a start point.

Turn left along this track and cross a bridge over the Allt na Ciste (the path of the return route emerges from the right here) then continue to a fork. Go right, then as the track loops left, turn right onto a path and cross the Allt Bàn by a bridge to rejoin the track on the other side of a ford. Continue to meet the track from the road end at Glenmore Lodge, then turn right along this. Now on the main track that travels north-east through Glenmore Forest, as followed by Meall a' Bhuachaille [2], continue along the floor of the glen

START & FINISH: Allt Bàn Car Park (NH981094); pay & display
DISTANCE: 13km; 8 miles
HEIGHT GAIN: 500m; 1640ft
APPROX TIME: 4-5hrs

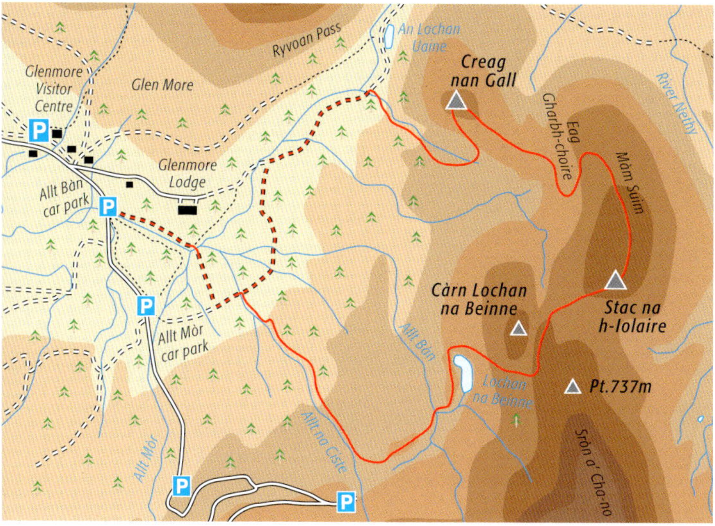

towards the Ryvoan Pass with the wooded slopes of Meall a' Bhuachaille and Creag nan Gall rising steeply on either side ahead.

The next section is not apparent! After about 900m, pass all obvious track entrances and paths (they lead nowhere) and cross a small burn that runs under the track to reach a wooden bench beneath a Scots pine. The route now strikes up the hillside here, through the undergrowth. However, before doing that, it is worth continuing for 400m to view idyllic An Lochan Uaine (the Little Green Loch).

Return to the bench, then 8m from it towards the lochan, go through a gap in the undergrowth and slant slightly left across grass with no real sign of a path. After 20m or so, a rough path will be found which, after about 100m, leads to a step over the small burn and a very steep but short ascent up the hillside. It is rough terrain but the path keeps going to emerge from the trees and reach a flat area with a moraine mound

41

Stac na h-Iolaire

Meall a' Bhuachaille from the flanks of Creag nan Gall

on its right side.

Leave the now vague path, cross the flat area leftwards and follow the trickle of a burn for 100m, then head up left to pick up a clear (but initially difficult to spot) route which slants leftwards up the heathery hillside. When this peters out higher up, continue through the heather past the odd boulder to reach the 632m summit, which is a fabulous little viewpoint from which to survey the Loch Morlich basin and the leading edge of the Northern Cairngorm massif.

Over to the left, a flat, grassy-looking shelf can be seen running across the hillside between the 570m and 580m

Creag nan Gall and Meall a' Bhuachaille from Stac na h-Iolaire

Stac na h-Iolaire

Eag a' Gharbh-choire meltwater channel

Glaciation
The last great ice sheet covered Scotland some 22,000 years ago and The Cairngorms abound in the classic features produced by the glacial shaping of the landscape; corries, glacial troughs; rock slope failures and associated boulder fields. They also display numerous landforms left behind by the retreating ice from some 13,000 years ago. On this walk you will see many such examples in Glen More and on its surrounding hillsides: moraine ridges & eskers (ridges of glacial deposition material), kames & kame terraces (deposition mounds and terraces), kettle holes (water-filled depressions created by blocks of ice and sediment) and meltwater channels (cut by water from melting ice), erratics (isolated boulders of different rock left by glaciers). In the Spey Valley itself, the small hills Kennapole Hill & Ord Bàn [19] *and* Torr Alvie [20] *are large-scale examples of roches moutonnees, rock formations created by the passage of a glacier.*

contours. This is a kame terrace and it indicates the level of the Glen More ice sheet where meltwater ponded against it. This feature can be followed across the Cairn Gorm access road and the hillside beyond, beneath the obvious notch of the Chalamain Gap.

One can imagine standing here above a vast ice sheet filling Glen More, the Loch Morlich and Rothiemurchus basin, and extending out to the Spey valley. Loch Morlich is a large kettle hole loch, left behind after the ice sheet receded, whilst the forests that surround it sit on glacial deposition.

Descend a rough path south-east towards Stac na h-Iolaire, which rises ahead with Bynack More looming large behind it. Beyond a large boulder, the path becomes vague but runs just below the crest to reach the col between the hills. This is the Eag a' Garbh-choire, a long, boulder-filled glacial meltwater channel, similar to the Chalamain Gap and Eag a' Chait encountered on Creag a' Chalamain [16], which can be seen to the south-west. Another channel, which runs in the same direction, can be seen above the kame terrace, 1km to the south.

Ascend the far side and slant left up the heathery slope to pick up a deer track and rough path that climbs onto the shoulder ahead, the Màm Suim.

Stac na h-Iolaire

Bynack More across Strath Nethy from Stac na h-Iolaire

Turn south and climb easily onto the long and flat crest of Stac na h-Iolaire (Cliff of the Eagle).

The 742m summit lies at the far end overlooking Strath Nethy where the flat ground terminates abruptly in a shallow but very steep corrie whose headwall cliff consists of curiously stacked flat rocks, beneath which there is an impressive scree slope. This too is as an outcome of glaciation and below can be seen the results of glacial deposition in the great trench of Strath Nethy.

On the opposite side of Strath Nethy, Bynack More and A' Chòinneach fill the view, with Beinn Mheadhoin framed between them and Cairn Gorm at the head of the strath. Closer at hand the Sròn a' Cha-no ridge, ascended by Cairn Gorm [6], lies ahead and forms the west side of the strath leading to Cnap Coire na Spreidhe and the summit of Cairn Gorm.

Descend south-west to a col (another overflow meltwater channel) then cross flat ground towards another meltwater channel over to the right. A rough path climbs up the left-hand side above this channel and is followed along its length to drop to the entrance at the far side. A short 30m ascent can be made up right onto Càrn Lochan na Beinne (692m), which is another splendid viewpoint.

From the entrance to the channel, continue on the path which now swings round to descend northwards across

Stac na h-Iolaire

Lochan na Beinne and Cairn Gorm

the slope. Lower down, what was a clear path disappears in heathery ground, which is descended to the north end of lovely little Lochan na Beinne. There is an interesting view across the loch, up Coire Laogh Mòr and Coire na Ciste, all the way to the summit of Cairn Gorm.

Follow a path along the west side of the loch to meet the path that runs between the Coire na Ciste car park and the Sròn a' Cha-no ridge, then follow this quite steeply downhill to cross the Allt Bàn, usually by a step over. Ascend an eroded peaty path onto, then along, a lateral moraine ridge, with fine views to Meall a' Bhuachaille and the **Kincardineshire Hills** [1], and continue to reach the side of the Allt na Ciste.

Turn right and follow a rough path down beside the burn into the forest. Although the path is boggy in places it provides a pleasant route that is most definitely well off the beaten track. A short way in, go straight across a flat boggy area, and much further down, watch for the point where the path nears the burn then drops down a steep slope to gain the path alongside it. In a further 350m the path emerges onto the track used in the initial approach. Turn left along this and follow it back to the start.

Creag nan Gall from the flanks of Càrn Lochan na Beinne

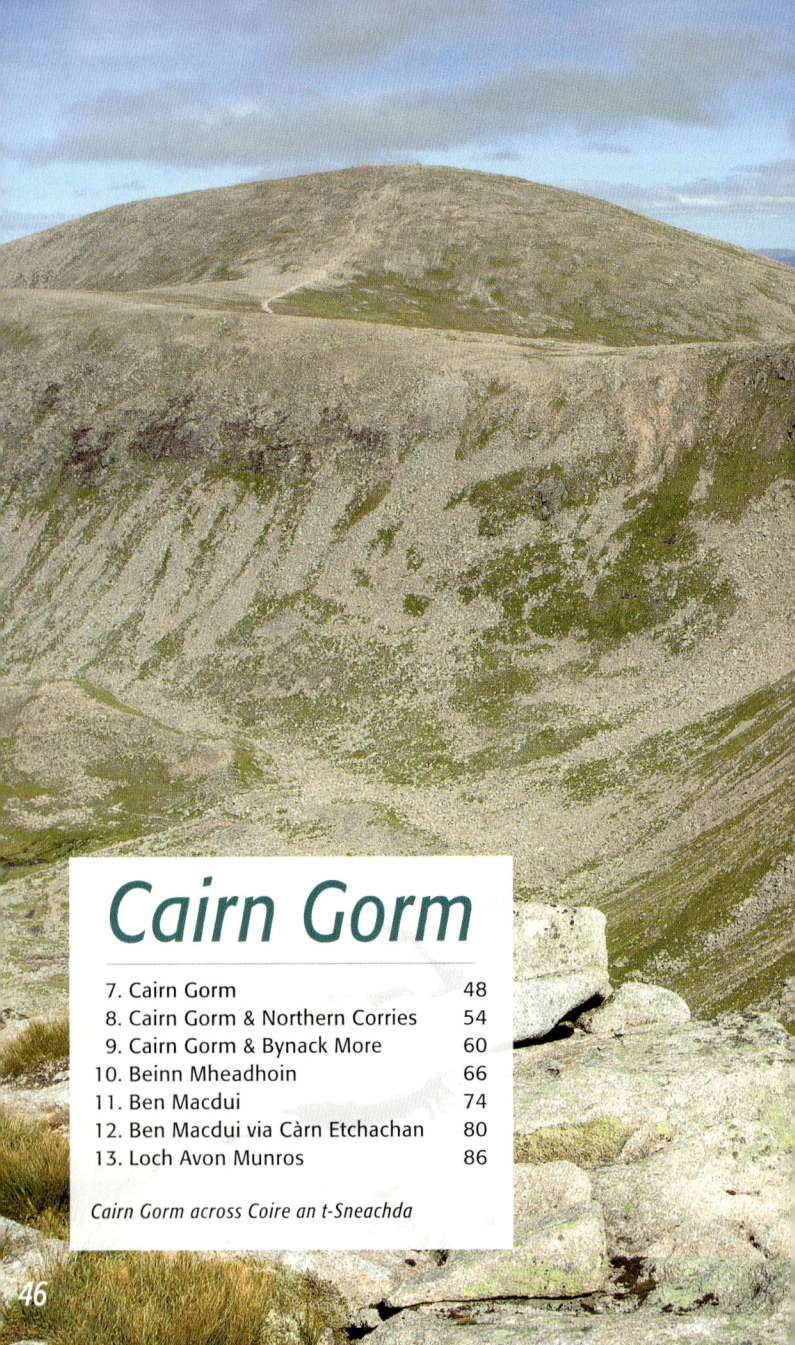

Cairn Gorm

7. Cairn Gorm	48
8. Cairn Gorm & Northern Corries	54
9. Cairn Gorm & Bynack More	60
10. Beinn Mheadhoin	66
11. Ben Macdui	74
12. Ben Macdui via Càrn Etchachan	80
13. Loch Avon Munros	86

Cairn Gorm across Coire an t-Sneachda

7 Cairn Gorm
Britain's sixth highest mountain

Cairn Gorm and Coire Cas across Loch Morlich

Although the lowest of the five Cairngorm 4000 foot mountains, Cairn Gorm has given its name to the entire massif, no doubt due to its prominence in the view from Speyside. Its great domed shape rises above the big but shallow corrie bowl of Coire Cas, which together with the two rock-crowned Northern Corries to the west, forms the distinctive northern edge of this great massif. Cairn Gorm is most easily climbed from Coire Cas, which holds the principal infrastructure for the Cairngorm Mountain Ski Centre.

However, a much more satisfactory route is from the lesser known Coire na Ciste, via the mountain's unfrequented easternmost ridge, Sròn a' Cha-no, which provides a fantastic off the beaten track approach.

The route begins from the Coire na Ciste car park, off to the left on the access road to Coire Cas. Skiing used to take place in Coire na Ciste (Corrie of the Deep Narrow Shape) but practically all the low level infrastructure has been removed.

Walk towards a disused building, then

START & FINISH: Coire na Ciste Car Park (NH998074); voluntary path maintenance donation
DISTANCE: 11km; 7 miles
HEIGHT GAIN: 780m; 2560ft
APPROX TIME: 4–5hrs

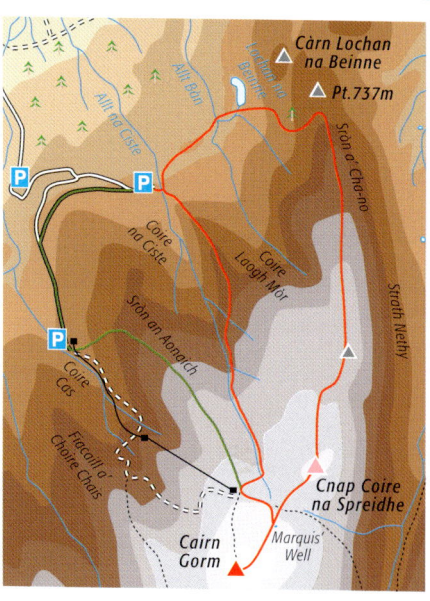

go through a gap in the bushes to drop down a wooden staircase and cross a bridge over the Allt na Ciste, the fast-flowing burn that cuts its course through the corrie. Take the path on the left for a short distance, before bearing right at a fork to continue across heather-clad moorland; bog cotton and bog asphodel scatter the ground, which can be a little marshy. Ahead on the skyline is the ridge of Sròn a' Cha-no.

Either go left around a morraine mound or over it, with fine views to the **Kincardineshire Hills** [1] and **Meall a' Bhuachaille** [2], then drop to the Allt Bàn. Once over this small burn the rough path climbs past little Lochan na Beinne, then steeply up the hillside towards some isolated stands of pine. Traverse right beneath the trees then up their right side on heather slopes as the incline increases again. Either continue to the shallow col at 721m overlooking Strath Nethy, or take a rough path just before it, which

Lochan na Beinne

49

Cairn Gorm

Stac na h-Iolaire (right) and the Sròn a' Cha-no ridge

heads up right onto the ridge.

A narrow but good path now climbs south up the crest of the Sròn a' Cha-no ridge. To the north is **Stac na h-Iolaire** [6], the Abernethy Forest and Speyside whilst to the east, Bynack Beg and **Bynack More** [4] lie across the deep trench of Strath Nethy. It is the steepest bit of the ridge and when the gradient eases, superb easy walking leads across heathery ground, scattered with small boulders. The ridge runs above the shallow bowls of Coire Laogh Beag and Coire Laogh Mòr; Small Corrie of the Calf and Big Corrie of the Calf.

Pass over a little rocky rise and continue across pathless level ground carpeted with luxurious moss. There is a good chance of spotting mountain hare darting across this wild and little frequented place, as well as small flocks of snow bunting and ptarmigan. Cross another little rocky rise and continue to the squat granite tor, which at 1028m marks the end of this section; there is a grand view of **Beinn Mheadhoin** [10] to the south.

The continuing ridge lies over to the right, reached across more mossy, flat terrain. Now much broader, the ridge leads onto a granite-topped crest with a

Stac na h-Iolaire from Sròn a' Cha-no

Cairn Gorm

The Sròn a' Cha-no ridge

final rise south soon gaining the 1150m granite tor of Cnap Coire na Spreidhe (Knob Above the Cattle Corrie); a Munro Top (see p5).

An extensive panorama takes in Cairn Gorm, Beinn Mheadhoin, Beinn a' Bhuird, Bynack More, Ben Rinnes and the Moray Coast. It is worth detouring 100m or so to the east, to a cairned outcrop on the very edge, to admire the steep drop and boulder-fields falling into Strath Nethy.

Descend west then swing round across a broad saddle above the shallow bowl of Ciste Mhearad to reach the ski tow at the head of Coire na Ciste. The nicely engineered Marquis' Well Path is then met coming up from the Ptarmigan Station and followed steadily uphill past the spring itself; named after one of the Marquises of Huntly. At a height of 1190m, it is one of a number of high mountain springs in the massif. The great domed top of Cairn Gorm is soon gained at a mast and stone-enclosed weather station, where a large cairn 50m to the north-west marks the 1244m highpoint

The summit weather station is operated by Heriot Watt University and has been taking weather data since 1977. Having to cope with extremes of

Bynack More from the ascent to Cnap Coire na Spreidhe

Cairn Gorm

Weather station on the summit of Cairn Gorm

weather, particularly incredibly low temperatures, means its instruments are housed in a heated cylinder, only being briefly exposed for half hourly readings. The highest wind speeds in the UK have been recorded here; 173mph (278kph) in March 1986 and 176mph (283kph) in January 1993.

As you would expect from Britain's sixth highest mountain, the outlook is superb, taking in almost all of the principal mountains of the Cairngorm National Park, together with much of north and north-eastern Scotland. On a clear day, Lochnagar can be seen to the south-east, whilst westwards beyond the Northern Corries, some 55 miles (90km) away, Ben Nevis pokes up between Aonach Mòr and Aonach Beag. To make the most of the extensive views you may have to wander around the summit area a bit.

The best descent is to return via the Marquis' Well Path, swinging left to gain the Ptarmigan Station at the top of the ski-centre's uplift facilities. The other option via the 'tourist path' is marginally more direct, but less pleasant. This descends directly north to the Ptarmigan Station, on a path initially

Snow Bunting
A small population of this rare arctic specialist resides on the high tops of the Cairngorms. Chances of spotting them are increased in the winter when migratory birds fly south from Iceland and Scandinavia and they can be seen in flocks. Sparrow-sized, with a distinctive white underbelly, the Snow Bunting nests in rock crevices on open mountain slopes.

Cairn Gorm

lined with cairns, then surfaced with cobblestones, which can be uncomfortable to walk on, especially in descent. The path is also lined with wooden posts and roped-in to protect the fragile habitat. If you do choose this route, please keep to the path.

The Ptarmigan is Britain's highest restaurant but at the time of writing it is closed due to the shutdown of the funicular railway. When open, walkers are able to access the facility and even take the train down; it is not permissible to get the up train and leave the building to access the hill though. There are now two alternatives for the descent from the Ptarmigan.

Ptarmigan Station and Loch Morlich

The first is to go around the right side of the station and descend the well-constructed Windy Ridge Path (ascended by Cairn Gorm & Northern Corries [8]). This initially goes down the left side of the snow fences on the crest of the broad ridge of Sròn an Aonaich to reach the Coire Cas car park. It provides a comfortable and speedy descent with fine views over Coire Cas to the Northern Corries, as well as over Loch Morlich and the Glenmore Forest to Aviemore and Speyside. However, to regain the Coire na Ciste car park there is 2.5km of road and verge walking.

The second is a more direct alternative. This follows a track through the snow fences past the top of the West Wall Poma Lift then under the Coire na Ciste T-bar ski tow to the start of the Ptarmigan T-bar where the Allt na Ciste is crossed to descend its grassy right bank. Initially vague, the path becomes distinct just below the level of the start of the ski tow on the opposite side. Crossing a tributary, the path then traverses downhill onto the right-hand ridge of Creagan Dubh (followed in ascent by Cairn Gorm & Bynack More [9]), which is descended with good views across Loch Morlich to regain the Coire na Ciste car park.

Beinn Mheadhoin, Loch Etchachan and Càrn Etchachan from Cairn Gorm's summit

8 Cairn Gorm & Northern Corries
The edge of the massif

Cairn Gorm – Coire Cas, Coire an t-Sneachda and Coire an Lochain

One of the finest walks in The Cairngorms, this route starts from the Coire Cas car park at a height of 630m. Ascending to the summit of Cairn Gorm, it then traverses westwards along the tops of Coire an t-Sneachda and Coire an Lochain with an optional ascent of Creag an Leth-choin (Lurcher's Crag), before a return out in front of the corries, hopefully lit-up by the sun.

Head between the funicular Base Station and the Day Lodge to go up the road beneath the funicular tracks, then break off left on the signposted Windy Ridge Path. This expertly constructed path rises quite steeply north-east then south-east up the lower slopes of the Coire Cas bowl. The view behind across the Glenmore Forest Park to Loch Morlich and the long ridge of the **Kincardineshire Hills** [1] and **Meall a' Bhuachaille** [2] is very fine. Over to the right, the cliffs of the Northern Corries dominate the view and provide a welcome alternative from the ski paraphernalia. The incline eases a little as the broad stony ridge of Sròn an Aonaich (Promontory of the High Moorland Ridge) is gained and the path swings south towards Cairn Gorm's summit dome and the Ptarmigan Station.

In good visibility it is better to avoid the cobblestone surfaced route to the top, which has also been roped-in to

START & FINISH: Coire Cas Car Park (NH985074); parking charge
DISTANCE: 11km; 7miles
HEIGHT GAIN: 810m; 2657ft
APPROX TIME: 4–5hrs

help prevent erosion of the fragile habitat. Instead, take the track and path uphill on the left immediately before the 'tourist path'. This is the Marquis' Well Path, which gives a more pleasant ascent, initially between the snow fences to just before the Ptarmigan T-bar ski tow where **Cairn Gorm** [7] via the Sròn a' Cha-no ridge joins, then turning south towards the summit.

If there is a desire to take-in all four of Cairn Gorm's subsidiary Munro Tops (see p5), two are en route anyway, then break-off the path here and cross the saddle between Coire na Ciste and Ciste Mhearad to the east to gain the top of Cnap Coire na Spreidhe (1150m). This granite-topped outlier overlooks Strath Nethy, with A' Chòinneach and Bynack More beyond. A 100m detour to a cairned outcrop on the edge is worthwhile, to admire the steep drop and boulder fields falling into Strath Nethy. Return the same way

Cnap Coire na Spreidhe

Cairn Gorm & Northern Corries

The Windy Ridge path up Sron an Aonaich

then continue, which adds about 25mins to the overall walk.

Ascend past the Marquis' Well spring to gain the flat top of the mountain and continue to a mast and stone-enclosed weather station (see p52). The 1244m highpoint is marked by a large cairn 50m to the north-west. The panorama is extensive, but to make the most of it you may have to wander around a bit.

The Northern Corries can now be seen, together with the top of the Fiacaill a' Choire Chais ridge to the west, marked by a large cairn. Leave the summit near the weather station and descend gravelly ground to gain the path below, then follow this round beneath the top of the Fiacaill a' Choire

Loch Morlich from the summit

Cairn Gorm & Northern Corries

Chais to reach a shallow dip on the edge of Coire an t-Sneachda. A short climb up the edge gains the top of Stob Coire an t-Sneachda (1176m); a Munro Top.

Continue westwards, dropping to the col with Cairn Lochan where a path known as the Goat Track descends into Coire an t-Sneachda. The route from **Beinn Mheadhoin** [10] arrives here via Coire Domhain on the left, then goes down the Goat Track into Coire an t-Sneachda. Climb the slope ahead, swinging up right on the path towards the top of the Fiacaill Buttress to reach the cliff edge then go left to the top of Cairn Lochan (1215m), another Munro Top; the view down into Coire an Lochan and beyond to Creag an Leth-choin is wonderful. The summit is the second of two high-points, perched on the edge of the cliffs on the far side of a gully named The Vent, which bites into the rim.

Coire an t-Sneachda from Cairn Gorm

Cairn Gorm & Northern Corries

Cairn Gorm and Stob Coire an t-Sneachda

Descend westwards along the edge, then away from it, on a path that crosses the head of the Allt Coire an Lochain by stepping stones to meet the main path to and from **Ben Macdui** [11] on Miadan Creag an Leth-choin; the long ridge which runs down the west side of the corrie. There are now two options. The first simply continues on this path, which traverses across onto the ridgeline then down it.

The second leaves the main path to head north-west down to a saddle, then make the short ascent onto Creag an Leth-choin (1053m), known as Lurcher's Crag (see p79), another

---

Coire an t-Sneachda & Coire and Lochain
These two corries with their sensational cliffs are known as the Northern Corries, and together with the summit of Cairn Gorm and Coire Cas they present the distinctive northern rampart of the Central Cairngorm Plateau, which overlooks Loch Morlich and catches the eye from the Spey Valley beyond. Lying to the west of Cairn Gorm and Coire Cas, Coire an t-Sneachda is separated from Coire an Lochain by the Fiacaill Coire an t-Sneachda (simply known as the Fiacaill Ridge), which holds the Fiacaill Buttress.

Facing north, the floors of both corries lie above the 900m contour and top-out at around 1200m, which means they are subjected to the extremes of weather. When combined with the lack of winter sunlight, this means that snow and ice can accumulate at any time from late September and last well into spring.

This snow holding capacity and their accessibility from the Coire Cas car park means the Northern Corries are the most popular winter climbing destination in Britain and as a result they can be very busy at that time of the year.

Coire an t-Sneachda translates as Corrie of the Snow while Coire an Lochain simply means Corrie of the Small Loch, relating to the small lochan in its base.

Cairn Gorm & Northern Corries

Càrn Eilrig, the Làirig Ghru and Creag an Leth-choin from Cairn Lochan

Munro Top, perched on the edge of the Làirig Ghru. Return towards the saddle, then either go down the shallow corrie to the north to pick up a vague path that leads around the base of the long ridge, or contour out onto the ridge and follow the main path down. This adds about 25mins to the overall walk.

Both options meet after crossing the Allt Coire an Lochain where the good path is followed north-east across the Allt Coire an t-Sneachda to the start.

Coire Domhain and Càrn Etchachan from Cairn Lochan

9 Cairn Gorm & Bynack More
Across Strath Nethy

Ascending Cairn Gorm from the Coire na Ciste car park, via the Creagan Dubh path and Cnap Coire na Spreidhe, this route then descends to The Saddle at the head of Strath Nethy above Loch Avon. Bynack More is then climbed via A' Chòinneach, followed by a descent over Bynack Beg into Strath Nethy, which is crossed to climb over the foot of the Sròn a' Cha-no ridge to regain the car park.

Walk towards the disused building at the far corner of the car park then go through a gap in the bushes to drop down a wooden staircase and cross a bridge over the Allt na Ciste, the burn that cuts through Coire na Ciste (Corrie of the Deep Narrow Shape). Turn right (left is the return and also the start for

START & FINISH: Coire na Ciste Car Park (NH998074); voluntary path maintenance donation
DISTANCE: 18km; 11 miles
HEIGHT GAIN: 1360m; 4462ft
APPROX TIME: 7–8hrs

Cairn Gorm and Cnap Coire na Spreidhe from A' Chòinneach

the ascent of **Cairn Gorm** [7] via the Sròn a' Cha-no ridge) and follow the path up the east side of Coire na Ciste, then along the Creagan Dubh ridge above the craggy slope that drops steeply into the corrie.

At a vague fork, where the principal path traverses right off the ridgeline towards the burn, go left and maintain a south-easterly ascent up the slope, passing through a gap in an old snow fence. Higher up, swing right up the broad ridge to gain the top of Cnap Coire na Spreidhe (Knob Above the Cattle Corrie); the north-eastern Munro Top (see p5) of Cairn Gorm, whose summit is marked with slabs of cream and pink coloured granite.

Make a slight descent to the west, then traverse across the broad saddle

Cairn Gorm & Bynack More

Bynack More from Ciste Mhearad

above Ciste Mhearad to reach the top of the Ptarmigan T-bar ski tow at the head of Coire na Ciste. On the far side of this, an engineered path coming up from the Ptarmigan Station is met and followed uphill past the Marquis' Well spring at an altitude of 1190m; named after one of the Marquises of Huntly, possibly the 5th Duke of Gordon (see p129) who frequented this spot.

The flat roof of the mountain is soon gained at a mast and weather station with Cairn Gorm's 1244m highpoint being marked by the large cairn 50m to the north-west. The panorama from Britain's sixth highest mountain is superb, with the majority of the big mountains in the surrounding Cairngorms National Park on show.

Return down the Marquis' Well Path towards the Ptarmigan T-bar tow, then turn right and cross pathless ground to drop into Ciste Mhearad. This small high-level hanging corrie sits above a steep slope which drops into Strath Nethy and holds snow well into spring. In winter it is used as an avalanche forecasting site and a good location used by snow craft instructional courses for digging snowholes.

A path descends to the right of the burn before turning south to make a descending traverse of Cairn Gorm's eastern slopes, crossing another burn then a boulder field before dropping to The Saddle at the head of Strath Nethy. This extraordinary location, one of the remotest in the National Park, is dominated by beautiful Loch Avon with the cliffs of Creag Dhubh and Beinn Mheadhoin's huge bulk filling the view on the far side.

Cross The Saddle and ascend the broad ridge ahead, on a path that rises gradually north-east through some rocky terrain passing some lovely small lochans. In a while the path fades, with the final approach turning north onto the elongated crest of A' Chòinneach over grassy slopes; there are splendid

Cairn Gorm & Bynack More

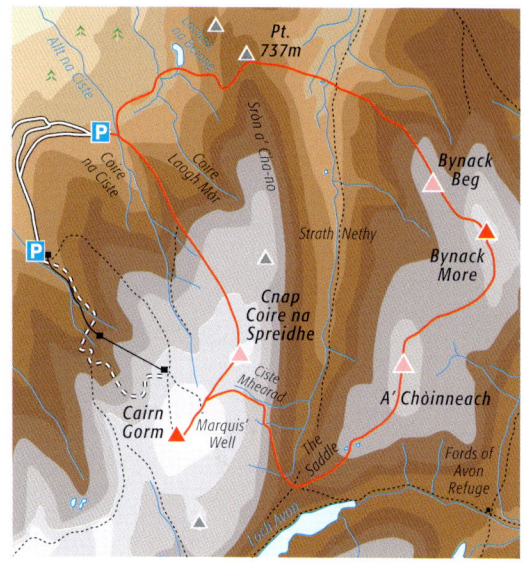

views behind along the length of Loch Avon to Càrn Etchachan and the Shelter Stone Crag with Ben Macdui beyond. The 1016m summit of this Munro Top (see p5) is marked by a small cairn, with Bynack Beg and Bynack More laid out beyond.

Head north then north-east and descend over spongy, grassy ground that flattens to a marshy plateau at 940m, home to mosses and wildflowers. In poor visibility, navigating across the featureless terrain requires care. However, in clear weather it is a steady but simple ascent east onto the broad ridge, then north to the Little Barns of Bynack, a small group of granite tors. The larger and more impressive Barns of Bynack stand a little lower to the east and are worth a

Beinn Mheadhoin and The Saddle from the Ciste Mhearad path

Cairn Gorm & Bynack More

Bynack More from A' Choinneach

visit. An easy climb north gains Bynack More's granite-bristling 1090m summit and an exemplary view; Ben Avon, Beinn a' Bhuird, Cairn Gorm and Meal a' Bhuachaille are all prominent.

Go along the crest a short way and descend north-west on a faint path to a shallow col. From there, an easy ascent gains the minor tor-topped Bynack Beg (970m), the second of Bynack More's Munro Tops, where the view of Strath Nethy far below grabs your attention. From here the route takes on an altogether different guise, crossing some steep, rough and remote ground. A path drops down Bynack Beg's north-west shoulder between the deep bowls of Coire Dearg and Coire Dubh (Red Corrie and Black Corrie). Initially the descent is gradual, but lower down it

Mountain Hare
Native to Britain, mountain hares shelter in shallow indentations in the ground (usually heather) known as forms. Perfectly adapted to their surroundings, mountain hare's powerful hind legs propel them to speeds of around 70kph. Their thick coat turns pure white in winter (with only their ear tips black), changing, in late spring, to grey-brown, providing superb camouflage from predators. They are smaller than their brown hare cousins (which are rarely found above 400m), with smaller ears to prevent excessive heat loss, in this harsh, arctic habitat.

Cairn Gorm & Bynack More

Bynack Beg and Bynack More across Strath Nethy

steepens and passes through awkward heathery ground before gaining the flat floor of lonely Strath Nethy.

Boots are likely to get wet as you head west over soft, marshy ground to cross the River Nethy, passing to the north of a small lochan. Any problems are short-lived though, as firm ground on the far side gives a steady climb up grassy, heathery slopes on a rough but improving path, beneath Stac na h-Iolaire (Steep Hill of the Eagle). The northern end of Cairn Gorm's Sron a' Cha-no ridge is gained at a 721m col.

Drop down the other side on a rough path, passing to the left of some isolated stands of trees then traversing beneath them before descending past the south end of little Lochan na Beinn with fine views to **Meall a' Bhuachaille** [2] and the **Kincardineshire Hills** [1]. Continue south-west out in front of Coire Laogh Mòr, crossing the Allt Bàn, to reach the side of the Allt na Ciste, then gain the bridge and staircase leading back to the car park.

Meall a' Bhuachaille from Lochan na Beinne

10 Beinn Mheadhoin
Middle Mountain

Beinn Mheadhoin and Loch Avon from the Coire Domhain path

Translated as Middle Mountain due to its location in the centre of the northern Cairngorm massif, the Munro of Beinn Mheadhoin (pronounced Ben Vane) is a tricky one to get to as it lies some distance from the nearest road. Rising high above Loch Avon, this mountain outlier is conspicuous by the granite tors on its summit crest.

Whilst it can be approached from the south, the better and more popular

Beinn Mheadhoin and Loch Avon from the Coire Raibeirt path

START & FINISH: Coire Cas Car Park (NH989060); parking charge
DISTANCE: 18km; 11 miles
HEIGHT GAIN: 1400m; 4600ft
APPROX TIME: 7–8hrs

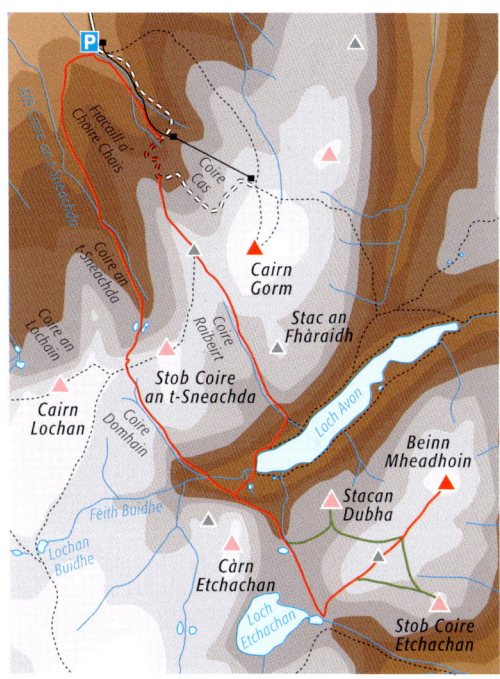

approach is from the north, starting from the Coire Cas car park on Cairn Gorm. This route gains the mountain by the Fiacaill a' Choire Chais, then drops into the spectacular Loch Avon basin by way of Coire Raibeirt. The return is made via Coire Domhain and the Goat Track into Coire an t-Sneachda.

From the Coire Cas car park, descend the wide track right of the Day Lodge then go left onto the waymarked Coire Cas Mountain Trail. This path climbs steadily south-east into Coire Cas (Steep Corrie), which is flanked on the left by the Sròn an Aonaich ridge and on the right by the Fiacaill a' Choire Chais, with the dome of Cairn Gorm ahead.

At a fork, keep right and continue to an access track just west of the Shieling Ski Station. Turn right and follow the track as it sweeps left then right. After it veers left for a second time, take a path on the right and make a gradual ascent to gain the Fiacaill a' Choire Chais (Narrow Ridge of the Steep Corrie).

Climb more steeply south along this defined ridge with superb views behind to Loch Morlich, **Kincardineshire Hills** [1] and **Meall a' Bhuachaille** [2]. The ridge culminates on the Cairngorm plateau beside a massive cairn at the head of Coire Raibeirt (Robbie's Corrie) with Beinn Mheadhoin beyond.

Descend steadily south-east, crossing the path off the summit of Cairn Gorm, as used by **Cairn Gorm & Northern Corries** [8] to reach a path beside the Allt Coire Raibeirt. Initially easy-angled, this well-travelled path steepens lower down where it runs beside the cascading burn, passing several beautiful waterfalls, with fine views south over Loch Avon to Beinn Mheadhoin.

About 250m above the lochside path, at a widening below a waterfall, ford the burn to a path on the other side and make a descending traverse

Beinn Mheadhoin

Beinn Mheadhoin's summit crest

south-west towards the southern tip of Loch Avon. The loch is reached at the sandy shoreline below the junction of the three burns; the Allt Coire Domhain, Fèith Buidhe and combined Garbh Uisge Beag and Garbh Uisge Mòr which pour down from the upper plateau into the basin.

Loch Avon is a stunning body of water enclosed by cliffs, with the impressive An Sticil (Shelter Stone Crag) on the right then Càrn Etchachan and overlooking the loch itself Stacan Dubha. Deep within the Cairngorms it is an astonishing location.

The surest and safest option to cross the burn flowing into the loch is by paddling the shallows of the loch, which are rarely above knee depth at the inflow. There are stepping stones here which are often clear.

The aim is to now ascend the obvious path that rises diagonally south-east up the hillside beneath Càrn Etchachan. Reach this by following a path to the right past a small lochan, towards the boulders beneath Shelter Stone Crag.

Higher, the path swings south beside the Allt nan Stacan Dubha to leave the basin, crossing one short, boggy section on flat ground to reach Loch Etchachan; a beautiful, isolated body of water thought to mean Loch of the Juniper.

At the eastern end, beside the outflow from Little Loch Etchachan, take a path uphill on the left. At times eroded, this zigzags steeply up Beinn Mheadhoin's south-western slopes, but soon the gradient lessens and a fainter path gains the 1163m western tor of the Barns of Beinn Mheadhoin.

A vast plateau, that is a joy to walk, extends north-east to the summit of Beinn Mheadhoin (1182m). This is

Beinn Mheadhoin

Across the deep glacial trench of the Làirig an Laoigh to the east (see p36) is Beinn a' Chaorain, seeming to merge with the vastness of Beinn a' Bhuird beyond. Then in a counter clockwise arc are Bynack More, Cairn Gorm, then Ben Macdui, with Braeriach beyond to its right, and Derry Cairngorm and Deeside to its left.

Beinn Mheadhoin has two outlying Munro Tops (see p5). Stob Coire Etchachan (1082m) lies to the south-east of the ascent path and, if required, can be picked up from there after a short descent. Stacan Dubha (1014m) lies to the north-west, with a fine view of Loch Avon, and is best picked up on the descent, crossing some rough ground to gain it and rejoin the approach path north of Loch Etchachan.

Retrace your steps to the Loch Avon basin. On nearing the basin floor, at a fork, go down left between some large boulders to a junction. From there, a path on the left climbs to the massive Shelter Stone boulder (see p84), which sits in the boulder field beneath the impressive Shelter Stone Crag.

formed by a granite tor almost 10m in height, the far north side of which offers the easiest ascent with one slightly awkward step. The elevated position heightens the stunning views.

Continue down to the Fèith Buidhe where crossing the burn can be problematic when it is running high. There

Cairn Gorm from Beinn Mheadhoin

Beinn Mheadhoin

are crossing points here, or lower down, and it is also possible to cross by boulder-hopping above where the burns meet. The other option is to return to wade the shallows of the loch as on the approach and go up the other side.

An excellent path to the right of the Allt Coire Domhain's cascading waters gives a very steep ascent of 300m in height, passing Hell's Lum Crag on the left and Stag Rocks on the right, to gain Coire Domhain (Deep Corrie, which is odd given its shallow nature!). The floor of the corrie is crossed in a north westerly direction over pathless montane

Ptarmigan
This wonderful hardy bird inhabits the high mountain areas of the Scottish Highlands, with the Cairngorm plateau providing an ideal habitat. Closely related to the more common grouse, ptarmigan change their plumage during the year, enabling them to merge perfectly into their surroundings. Their feathers turn pure white during winter, when the high tops are thick with snow, while during the summer months a more mottled appearance camouflages them against rocks and boulders.

Ptarmigan are also feathered from top to toe, allowing them to live in the extreme conditions of the Scottish mountains, keeping out the cold as they scrape about for food and dig snow holes that shield them from the biting winds and driving snow. They are resident birds, rarely moving far from where they breed, albeit that in the severest cold weather they may move to the forest edge.

Beinn Mheadhoin

Beinn Mheadhoin's summit tor

heath, and at times marshy ground, to reach the 1111m col between Cairn Lochan and Stob Coire an t-Sneachda. This is where the Goat Track starts; the path that drops into Coire an t-Sneachda.

The Goat Track is not recommended under snow unless suitably equipped, or when snows are melting, or even in heavy rain, as there can be rockfall. If in any doubt, climb east over Stob Coire an t-Sneachda, then north-east to the cairn at the top of Fiacaill a' Choire Chais and descend as for the approach.

However, in good conditions, zigzag down from the col via some steep and rocky ground where a little light scrambling may be required, albeit with no technical difficulty. Thereafter, make a descending traverse below the cliffs of what is called Fluted Buttress, towards the two little lochans that occupy the floor of Coire an t-Sneachda. It is a glorious natural amphitheatre, backed by the headwall cliffs that rise to Stob Coire an t-Sneachda.

Coire an t-Sneachda means Corrie of the Snow, an appropriate name as the cliffs are under winter's grip for much of the year (see p58). Pass between the two lochans and go carefully through a short section of boulder field to reach a good path. This leads out of the jaws of the corrie, between the Fiacaill Coire an t-Sneachda ridge on the left and the Fiacaill a' Coire Chais ridge on the right. Cross the Allt Coire an t-Sneachda and continue to join the path coming across from Coire an Lochain and Ben Macdui, then traverse across the foot of the Fiacaill a' Coire Chais back to the start.

Cairn Gorm, Bynack More and Loch Avon from Càrn Etchachan

11 Ben Macdui
Britain's Second Highest Mountain

Cairn Toul, Sgor an Lochain Uaine and Braeriach from Ben Macdui - distant Ben Nevis

Following her second trip to the summit of Ben Macdui in August 1860, Queen Victoria wrote in her diary *"The view at the top & from the cairn wonderfully fine & extensive, ranges & ranges of mountains, rising one behind the other like the waves of the sea & all so blue. We saw Ben Nevis quite distinctly, so that I could sketch it, & many other distant hills I cannot name."*

It certainly is a superb viewpoint, and with an excellent path running from Coire Cas out in front of The Northern Corries, almost all the way to the summit, Ben Macdui is accessible and therefore immensely popular. The summit is visited by thousands each year and whilst it is a relatively simple walk in good weather, it does penetrate deep into exposed, high-level, subarctic terrain. As a result, walkers should be suitably equipped and have the appropriate navigational skills to deal with conditions that can change quite rapidly from good to bad to make this quite a challenging undertaking.

Coire an Lochain from the approach

START & FINISH: Coire Cas Car Park (NH985074); parking charge
DISTANCE: 16km; 10 miles
HEIGHT GAIN: 720m; 2360ft
APPROX TIME: 5–6hrs

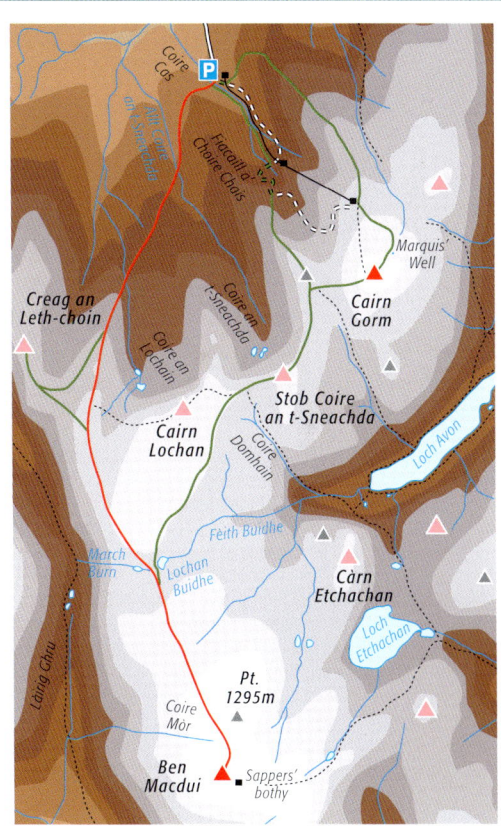

Leave the Coire Cas car park down the stepped path to the right of the Day Lodge building and cross the bridge over the Allt a' Choire Chais. After climbing a flight of steps, bear right along the well-constructed path that heads south-west. Already there are marvellous views across Rothiemurchus and towards Creag an Leth-choin.

When the path splits after 500m, keep right along heather-clad slopes with a fine view ahead to Coire an Lochain. The left-hand path leads into Coire an t-Sneachda and is the return from **Beinn Mheadhoin [10]** and **Ben Macdui via Càrn Etchachan [12]**. Soon stepping stones take you across the cascading waters of the Allt Coire an t-Sneachda, after which the path forks. Take the path on the right, which is flanked by lichen-encrusted boulders; the left-hand path heads up a stepped section towards Coire an Lochain. The path now climbs gradually up the hillside to cross the Allt Coire an Lochain then ascends steadily up the defined ridge of Miadan Creag an Leth-choin.

On the left Coire an Lochain is impressive, its cliffs dropping to the distinctive Great Slab, beneath which is the corrie floor, occupied by two lovely lochans. Large quantities of snow accumulate on the Great Slab and are regularly shed in avalanches which are known to pile into the lochan below. The corrie rim can become corniced and snow lingers here, and in Coire an t-Sneachda, long into the spring.

Soon flatter, more featureless ground

Ben Macdui

Coire an Lochain

is reached where a path descending from the top of Cairn Lochan gains the main path and the route passes a wet area at the source of the Allt Coire an Lochain. There is a remoter feel here, as you climb a little across the western slopes of Cairn Lochan, high above the Làirig Ghru. On the opposite side there is a fine view of Sròn na Làirige's slopes and the ridge ascended by Braeriach from the Sugarbowl [14].

The path now drops slightly to the plateau beyond, which is often described as a barren landscape. There is life here however, with ptarmigan, dotterel, mountain hare, snow bunting and maybe reindeer to be spotted (see p83); as well as lovely alpine flowers.

The path passes the watershed between Lochan Buidhe, which feeds Loch Avon, and a lochan feeding the March Burn, which falls into the Làirig Ghru to disappear before reaching the Pools of Dee. The March Burn (Allt na

Cairn Toul, Sgòr an Lochain Uaine and Braeriach

Ben Macdui

Cairn Lochain, Stob Coire an t-Sneachda and Cairn Gorm from Ben Macdui

Criche, the Stream of the Boundary) marks the old border between Strathspey and Deeside. When the weather is clear, a relatively simple walk continues, but there is featureless terrain and in poor visibility good navigational skills may be called on.

Although cairned, the route underfoot now becomes vague amongst the boulders that circle the lower slopes of Ben Macdui. Blocks of white quartz lie scattered about here, and the route that comes across from the col between Cairn Lochan and Stob Coire an t-Sneachda joins in at a large cairn on flatter ground in the boulder field. Beyond, the terrain improves and a clearer path rises up a steeper, gravelly section, then across the top of a shallow corrie named Coire Mòr, on easier-angled ground between unnamed Pt. 1295m and the summit dome.

Finally, a short rise leads through more boulders to the large cairn and elevated trig point that mark the summit of Ben Macdui (1309m) on an otherwise featureless flat table. Here there is one of the finest views within the Cairngorms National Park, that of the complex corries and ridges of Cairn Toul, Sgòr an Lochain Uaine (The Angel's Peak) and Braeriach, which is simply breathtaking.

On the west side of the cairn there is a viewpoint indicator which, although becoming difficult to read, does help identify some of the mountains that can be seen in the expansive views. The ruins of the Sappers' Bothy lie a short distance to the south-east, (see p78)

The simplest return is back the same way. However, a variation on this is to take the right-hand path between the two small lochans to gain the col between Cairn Lochan and Stob Coire an t-Sneachda. From there, go over Stob Coire an t-Sneachda to reach the large cairn at the top of the Fiacaill a'

Ben Macdui

Sappers' Bothy
Lying 150m to the south-east of Ben Macdui's summit cairn are the ruins of a small, roofless four-walled building known as the Sappers' Bothy. For many walkers this has acted as a welcome shelter from the elements and an aid to navigation. It is in fact what is called a Colby Camp, named after Thomas Colby who spent a full career working with the Ordnance Survey. An officer in the Royal Engineers (The Sappers) he was appointed by the OS to assist with the British Trigonometrical Survey which commenced in 1802. Working his way up the ladder, both in terms of rank and position within the OS, he led the Ordnance Survey's Trigonometrical Survey of Scotland, which was completed in 1852. He became one of the leading geographers of the day, as well as a Major General and a Director of the Ordnance Survey.

In order to carry out the triangulation surveys, camps were established at a number of strategic locations on the mountains by the Royal Engineers who also carried out the survey work. Due to the time required to take sightings and measurements in these remote locations, together the vagaries of the weather, a continuous presence by a number of 'sappers' over a period of time was required. Ben Macdui was thought to be the highest mountain in the country until the Ordnance Survey finally confirmed its height, and second place, in 1847.

When Queen Victoria ascended Ben Macdui on a pony for her first visit in October 1859, although she knew the correct height (still as it is today, interestingly), she was under the impression it was the highest; wishful thinking by her local guide perhaps!

Choire Chais ridge, then descend this ridge and the continuation path down Coire Cas. This only takes about 15min longer than returning by the route taken on the ascent.

Including Cairn Gorm is also a possibilty, descending via the Marquis' Well and Windy Ridge paths, as for the final section of the **Loch Avon Munros** [13]; the traverse of Ben Macdui, Beinn Mheadhoin and Cairn Gorm. This takes an additional 30mins or so to going down the Fiacaill a' Choire Chais ridge.

Another option is to return to NH976024 at the top of the Miadan Creag an Leth-choin ridge on the west side of Cairn Lochan. From there, leave the main path and descend north-west towards Creag an Leth-choin, its craggy top clearly visible ahead. Keep on as the ground drops to 997m, just above cliffs that drop abruptly into the Làirig Ghru, then ascend a path north through

Fiacaill a' Choire Chais

Ben Macdui

Creag an Leth-choin across the Làirig Ghru

more boulders onto the 1053m top of Creag an Leth-choin (Lurcher's Crag); a Munro Top (see p5). It is an impressive vantage point from which to gaze across the Làirig Ghru to Braeriach and Sgòran Dubh Mòr, as well as south to The Devil's Point at the far end.

The cliffs below the summit are popular with climbers, particularly during winter. The names of climbs, such as Blood Hound, Irish Wolfhound and Deerhound Ridge provide a link to Creag an Leth-choin's anglicised name of Lurcher's Crag, which comes from the tale of a number of hunting dogs that fell to their deaths from its summit having chased a stag there from Glen More.

Return to the main path down the Miadan Creag an Leth-choin ridge, which is then followed back as for the approach; the rough path in the corrie to the east can also be descended to join the main path after crossing the Allt Coire an Lochain. This adds about 25mins to the overall walk.

Kincardineshire Hills from Creag an Leth-choin

12 Ben Macdui via Càrn Etchachan
Loch Avon basin figure of eight

Beinn Mheadhoin, Càrn Etchachan and Shelter Stone Crag from the Coire Domhain path

Much of this route ignores the network of paths that criss-cross the Central Cairngorm Plateau. Instead it traverses some rough, pathless ground, leading well off the beaten track, to visit a remote, wild and inspiring landscape, granting an unforgettable figure of eight loop. A climb up the Fiacaill a' Choire Chais ridge gains the plateau from where it is on to the tops of Hell's Lum Crag, Shelter Stone Crag and Càrn Etchachan, followed by a traverse above Coire Etchachan to gain the summit of Ben Macdui. A descent to Loch Etchachan then Loch Avon, is followed by an unrelenting climb up Coire Domhain to regain the plateau and a return via Coire an t-Sneachda.

From the Coire Cas car park, descend the wide track right of the Day Lodge then go left onto the waymarked Coire Cas Mountain Trail. This path climbs steadily south-east into Coire Cas (Steep Corrie), which is flanked on the left by the Sròn an Aonaich ridge and on the right by the Fiacaill a' Choire Chais ridge, with the dome of Cairn Gorm ahead. Scotch argus and small heath butterflies may be spotted between June and September; also keep an eye out for ring ouzels (see p120) which are known to nest here.

At a fork, keep right and continue to an access track just west of the Shieling Ski Station. Turn right and follow the track as it sweeps left then right. After it veers left for a second time, take a path on the right and make a gradual ascent to gain the Fiacaill a' Choire Chais (Narrow Ridge of the Steep Corrie).

Climb more steeply south along this defined ridge with superb views behind to Loch Morlich, the **Kincardineshire Hills** [1] and **Meall a' Bhuachaille** [2]. The ridge culminates on the Cairngorm Plateau beside a massive cairn at the head of Coire Raibeirt with Beinn

START & FINISH: Coire Cas Car Park (NH985074); parking charge
DISTANCE: 21.5km; 13.5 miles
HEIGHT GAIN: 1330m; 4365ft
APPROX TIME: 7hrs 30mins –8hrs 30mins

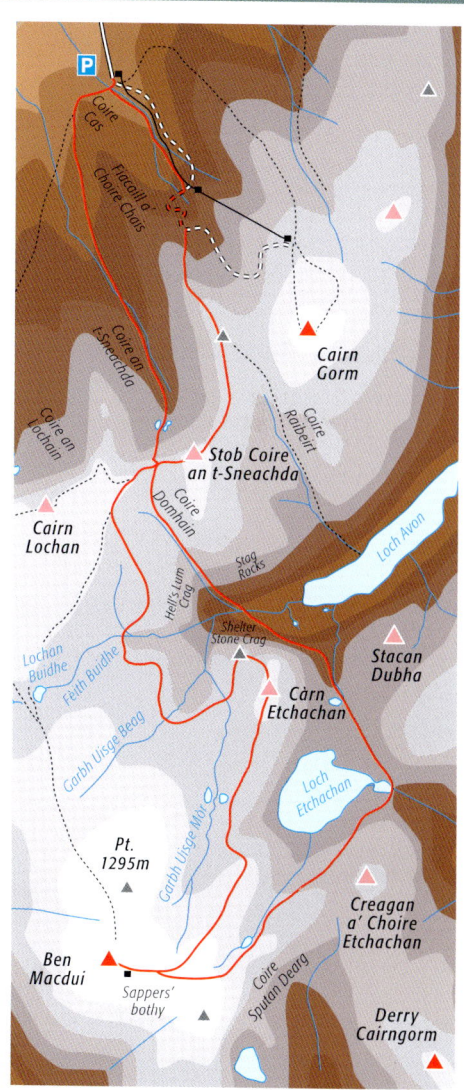

Mheadhoin beyond.

Continue south for 200m to meet the path coming off the summit of Cairn Gorm and follow this across a dip to ascend the lip of Coire an t-Sneachda (which can be snow corniced into the spring) onto Stob Coire an t-Sneachda. The magnificent panorama takes in Cairn Gorm, Ben Macdui and Derry Cairngorm.

Descend west, over rocky ground, to the 1111m col with Cairn Lochan at the head of Coire an t-Sneachda. On the return, the route arrives here from Coire Domhain on the left, then descends into Coire an t-Sneachda via a path called the Goat Track.

Take the clear path that rises gradually south-west across the flanks of Cairn Lochan and when it levels off after 600m, leave it and head south-east across flat montane heath onto an obvious rocky crest above Hell's Lum Crag; a superb vantage point high above the Loch Avon Basin.

For the next 5km the route is pathless and crosses a remote and wilder landscape, travelling above steep ground at times and alongside vertical cliffs. Real care must be taken, especially in poor weather when good

Ben Macdui via Càrn Etchachan

Càrn Etchachan across Loch Etchachan

navigation will be essential. However, its untamed nature improves the possibility of spotting mountain hare, snow bunting and dotterel (see p98).

Descend in a southerly direction, avoiding steep ground to the left, the rough terrain slowing progress. At the Fèith Buidhe, when water levels are low, feet may still get a little wet but when full of meltwater or in spate the crossing could be difficult. Once over, stay high across large shelves of rock before grassy slopes drop to the Garbh Uisge Beag, just above a waterfall.

After a reasonably simple crossing, climb steadily north-east over the faster flowing Garbh Uisge Mòr, then continue to the head of a cleft (Castlegates Gully) between Shelter Stone Crag and Càrn Etchachan. Bear left here for a

Shelter Stone Crag and Hell's Lum Crag

Ben Macdui via Càrn Etchachan

short climb onto the flat top of Shelter Stone Crag. At its edge the ground plummets 270m down into the Loch Avon basin whilst the outlook across Loch Avon is exceptional.

Return to the cleft and make the short, steep pull over boulders, near the cliff edge, onto Càrn Etchachan where there are further breathtaking views. The true summit of this outlying Munro Top (see p5) of Ben Macdui lies a little south. Beyond this, the wide ridge leads south-west above Loch Etchachan, passing over a minor rise on more rough ground and coming close to the Garbh Uisge Mòr. Once past some small pools, ascend onto the ridge on the left and rise steadily to meet the path coming up from Loch Etchachan.

By turning right up the path it is a gradual ascent onto Ben Macdui, with the final section across bouldery ground passing the ruin of the Sappers' Bothy (see p78). A large cairn and elevated trig point sit on the 1309m summit which provides a magnificent view that, on a clear day, stretches for at least 50 miles in all directions. Next to the cairn there is a viewpoint indicator which, although becoming difficult to read, does help identify some of the mountains that can be seen.

Retrace your steps and continue down the path to Loch Etchachan,

Reindeer
Forming the only free-ranging herd in Britain, reindeer may be spotted wandering languorously across the high ground of the Northern Cairngorms. They were introduced into the Cairngorms in 1952 by Swedish herder Mikel Utsi (the bridge across the Allt Mòr near the Sugarbowl car park being named after him) and his wife Dr Ethel Lindgren. From a small group of two bulls and five cows a healthy herd of 150 reindeer has been established. They are perfectly suited to life roaming the 10,000 acres of plateau and mountain top, their short summer coat thickening to a fleece during the winter months, while extra wide hooves prevent them from sinking in soft snow. Their favoured food includes cladonia lichen, which is prevalent on the higher ground of the Cairngorms.
Some reindeer are kept in an enclosure accessed from the Sugarbowl car park and the Cairngorm Reindeer Centre in Glenmore runs trips to see and feed them. The centre is interested in tracking the free-ranging herd and is happy to receive information on sightings, which can be done through their website.

Ben Macdui via Càrn Etchachan

through a remote and imposing arena to ford the outflow of Little Loch Etchachan where the broken cliffs of Càrn Etchachan are reflected in the loch.

Follow the main path northwards past that used to climb **Beinn Mheadhoin** [9] and traverse a short section of boggy ground alongside the Allt nan Stacan Dubha. The path then drops steeply into the breathtaking Loch Avon basin where there is an altogether different perspective to that given earlier from the surrounding heights.

Nearing the basin floor, at a fork, go down left between some large boulders to a junction. From there, a path on the left climbs to the Shelter Stone boulder. Continue down to the Fèith Buidhe, which can be awkward to cross (especially if running high), although crossing above where the three burns meet can provide easier passage. If wading footwear is carried it is easy to wade lower down where it is wider. If in any doubt, detour to paddle the shallows of the loch, which should always be easy.

An excellent path to the right of the Allt Coire Domhain's cascading waters gives a relentless 300m ascent, past Hell's Lum Crag, to gain Coire Domhain. There are superb views back to Loch Avon, Shelter Stone Crag and Càrn Etchachan. The gradient suddenly yields and the path rises gradually up the corrie by the placid waters to regain the col between Cairn Lochan and Stob Coire an t-Sneachda.

Descend north into Coire an t-Sneachda via the Goat Track, by the

Clach Dhion
Better known as the Shelter Stone, Clach Dhion (pronounced Clach Yeein') is, perhaps, the most famous refuge in the Cairngorms. It lies at the head of the Loch Avon basin, beneath the spectacular 270m high An Sticil (itself more commonly known as the Shelter Stone Crag) and has provided a sanctuary for walkers, climbers, soldiers and even Prime Ministers (Ramsey MacDonald apparently spent a night here) for over 200 years. The Cairngorm Club, the oldest and probably the largest climbing and hillwalking club in the country, was formed here in 1887 after the night of Queen Victoria's Golden Jubilee.

The shelter lies beneath a huge boulder said to weigh over 1500 tonnes, having fallen from An Sticil to fortuitously rest on four other boulders, creating a natural howff with an incredible view across Loch Avon. It has room (just) for around six people and its low roof provides it with a somewhat a claustrophobic feel. There are numerous other howffs under other boulders in the vicinity, illustrating just how popular overnighting in this wonderful place is.

Ben Macdui via Càrn Etchachan

Coire an t-Sneachda – the Goat Track can be seen coming down from the col

path that starts from the lowest point of the col. This is not recommended under snow unless suitably equipped, or when snows are melting, or even in heavy rain, as there can be rockfall. If in any doubt return over Stob Coire an t-Sneachda as for the approach.

Although the upper section of the Goat Track is quite steep there is never any real scrambling and several switchbacks make the going a little easier. The scenery is remarkable, with the cliffs of the Fiacaill Buttress over to the left and those of Fluted Buttress on the right, with Cairn Gorm beyond. The final section is a long traverse beneath the cliffs of Fluted Buttress where attention should be paid to possible rockfall from above.

On reaching the corrie floor, pass between two small lochans and go carefully through a short boulder field to reach a good path. This gives a pleasant and gradual descent out of the corrie, crossing the Allt Coire an t-Sneachda to go down and around the foot of the Fiacaill a' Choire Chais ridge to regain the start.

Evening light Coire an -t-Sneachda

13 Loch Avon Munros
Ben Macdui, Beinn Mheadhoin & Cairn Gorm

Ben Macdui across Loch Etchachan

Ascending the three principal Munros that make up this part of the high Cairngorm plateau, this challenging walk provides a superb and scenic outing. Aided by the excellent path network that connects these mountains, and given decent weather, it is an achievable target for most fit walkers. Starting from the Coire Cas car park, the plateau is gained by the path out in front of the Northern Corries which climbs around Cairn Lochan, as for the standard route to **Ben Macdui** [11]. From there, the route descends into the Loch Etchachan basin to climb Beinn Mheadhoin, before dropping into the spectacular Loch Avon basin where a tough ascent up Coire Raibeirt leads onto Cairn Gorm.

Leave the Coire Cas car park via the stepped path to the right of the Day Lodge and cross the bridge over the Allt a' Choire Chais. Climb a flight of steps, then bear right to follow the good path around the foot of the Fiacaill a' Choire Chais ridge to where it splits. Keep right to cross the Allt Coire an t-Sneachda on stepping stones and continue on the main path, ignoring one off to the left that leads into Coire an Lochain.

After crossing the Allt Coire an Lochain, follow the path onto the ridge that encloses the right-hand side of Coire an Lochain, the Miadan Creag an Leth-choin, with increasingly fine views into this impressively rocky corrie. Traverse round the western flanks of Cairn Lochan, high above the great through pass of the Làirig Ghru. Drop a little to the watershed and pass

START & FINISH: Coire Cas Car Park (NH985074); parking charge
DISTANCE: 23.5km; 14.5 miles
HEIGHT GAIN: 1500m; 4920ft
APPROX TIME: 8hrs 30mins –10hrs

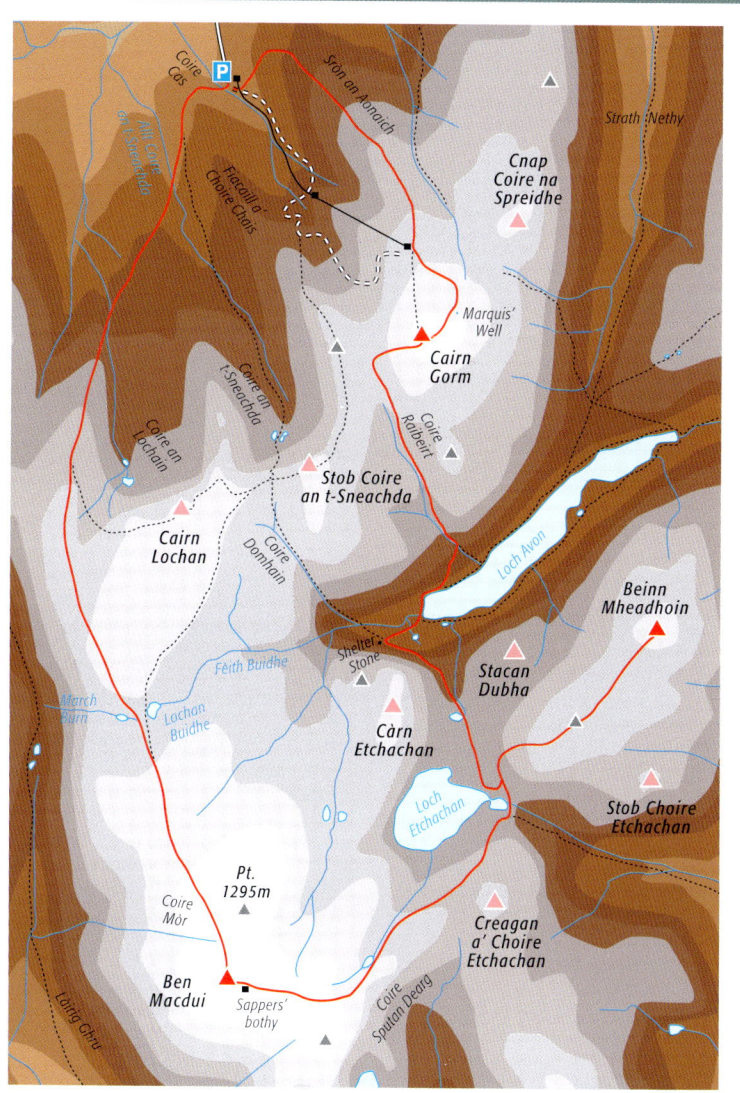

Loch Avon Munros

Cairn Gorm, Bynack More and Beinn Mheadhoin across Loch Etchachan

between two small lochans, then go through a boulder field on a slight rise to join the route coming across from the col between Cairn Lochan and Stob Coire an t-Sneadchda at a large cairn.

Continue on the path, up a steeper gravelly section, then across easier-angled ground at the top of a shallow corrie named Coire Mòr, between unnamed Pt. 1295m and the summit dome. Finally, a short rise leads onto the bouldery flat top of Ben Macdui where the summit trig point sits atop a large cairn. The view is superb and there is a viewpoint indicator next to the cairn. Albeit this is a bit worn, it should help identify many of the summits that can be seen.

Beinn Mheadhoin (pronounced Ben Vane), the next mountain on the traverse, is seen to the north-east. Walk south-east across pathless bouldery ground for 150m to reach the ruins of the Sappers Bothy (see p78), then head east to pick up a path on flat ground at the head of an open corrie to the north and a corrie to the north-east. In poor visibility care should be taken here, for the ground falls away in various directions. However, when clear the route is obvious. Follow the path east across the flat ground, then north-east to descend through a wonderfully wild landscape, dropping to gorgeous Loch Etchachan, over which there is a splendid view to Cairn Gorm. Continue to the outflow of Little Loch Etchachan which is a lovely spot to linger, with the loch, the highest sizeable body of water in the country, framed by Càrn Etchachan's steep cliffs.

Ford the Coire Etchachan Burn, which drops into Glen Derry to eventually feed the River Dee, and turn right uphill to begin the steep ascent onto Beinn Mheadhoin. The eroded path zigzags uphill, with fine views of Ben Macdui and Cairn Gorm unfolding. When the

Loch Avon Munros

incline eases, a fainter path leads to the western tor of the Barns of Beinn Mheadhoin at 1163m on the long summit plateau.

A gentle climb north-east crosses the huge summit plateau past other tors that can be visited to gain the highest tor marking the top of Beinn Mheadhoin. At nearly 10m in height this seemingly impregnable chunk of granite is very impressive. Fortuitously the tor tapers down at its north end and this offers the easiest line of ascent.

Whilst it is not a particularly difficult climb in the dry, there is a step left partway up that some may find awkward. The highest point contains two eroded potholes that are often water-filled and the elevated position serves to heighten the splendid viewing experience. Descend from the top and retrace your steps back to Little Loch Etchachan.

Turn right and walk north-west beneath the steep slopes of Càrn Etchachan. The path crosses one short section of wet ground alongside the Allt nan Stacan Dubha before it swings away from the burn to drop steeply into the Loch Avon basin. Almost completely encircled by the cliffs of Stacan Dubha, Càrn Etchachan, Shelter Stone Crag, Hell's Lum Crag, Stag Rocks and Stac an Fhàraidh, it is a breathtaking natural amphitheatre, down whose sides water pours into beautiful Loch Avon.

Near the floor of the basin, keep right at a fork and partway along a small lochan go left at another fork to reach the Fèith Buidhe. Cross the river (when levels are low it is reasonably simple), then follow a path to the stunning beach at the head of Loch Avon. Another option keeps right to gain the beach where the shallows at the inflow can either be crossed on stepping stones, or by a simple paddle; even

Loch Avon Munros

Cairn Gorm from the descent to Loch Avon

when the river is running high it is rarely deep. The route **Around Loch Avon** [5] arrives here along the south side of the loch on its way round the basin. It is a superb spot to stop awhile and revel in the extraordinary scenery, as well as prepare for the tough ascent to come!

On the far side of the beach, the quickest route is to take the upper path, which branches off almost immediately. Ascend diagonally up the hillside to ford the Allt Coire Raibeirt at a widening a short distance below a waterfall. The other route is to take the lower lochside path for 0.5km then, once across the outflow of the Allt Coire Raibeirt, turn left uphill; perhaps better if a lot of water is pouring into the basin. Either way, a path leads up the right side of the burn for an unremittingly steep ascent up Coire Raibeirt (Robbie's Corrie).

The well-constructed nature of this path helps the interesting ascent alongside a series of cascades and waterfalls, whilst the superb view back to Beinn Mheadhoin rising above the glistening waters of Loch Avon gives a good excuse for a breather. Eventually the angle relents and the landscape opens out as the plateau is reached again for a steadier rise up the head of the corrie.

Before reaching the large cairn that marks the top of the Fiacaill a' Choire Chais, turn right onto the link path between **Cairn Gorm & Northern Corries** [7] and begin the final ascent onto Cairn Gorm. The path is a little unclear in places as it ascends the stony and gravelly slope to arrive at the

Beinn Mheadhoin from Coire Raibeirt

Loch Avon Munros

Kincardineshire Hills from Cairn Gorm

mast and stone-enclosed weather station on the flat top of the mountain; a large cairn 50m to the north-west marks the 1244m highpoint. The panorama is superb, extending across a vast landscape; on a clear day Ben Nevis and the West Highlands can even be seen.

Unless the visibility is poor, avoid the obvious path to the north, which drops to the Ptarmigan Station. Initially lined with marker cairns, it is roped-in and flanked with wooden posts lower down and has a cobblestone surface that is awkward to walk on, especially in descent. Instead, head north-east from the weather station to pick up the nicely graded and surfaced Marquis' Well Path, which leads down past the spring itself before swinging round to the Ptarmigan Station.

Pass to the right of the station then follow the well-engineered Windy Ridge Path down the left side of the snow fences on the broad Sròn an Aonaich ridge, with further fabulous views, all the way back to the Coire Cas car park to end an immensely satisfying day.

Coire Cas and The Northern Corries from Sròn an Aonaich

Rothiemurchus

14. Braeriach from the Sugarbowl	94
15. Braeriach from Coylumbridge	100
16. Creag a' Chalamain	106
17. Càrn Eilrig	114
18. Creag Dubh	118
19. Kennapole Hill & Ord Bàn	122
20. Torr Alvie	126

Creag Dhubh above Loch an Eilein

14 Braeriach from the Sugarbowl
Bulky Braeriach

Braeriach's summit cliffs, Coire Bhrochain

Forming part of the Western Cairngorm Plateau, Braeriach is a huge mountain in every respect. Its bulky form dominates the northern edge of the Cairngorms where it presents a distinctive sight sitting between the Làirig Ghru to its east and the glacial trough of Gleann Eanaich to its west. Only Ben Nevis and Ben Macdui in the British Isles are loftier. Its vast summit plateau is home to the Wells of Dee, the source of the River Dee (the highest of any river in Britain), which ends its 87 mile (140km) journey in the North Sea at Aberdeen.

To its south, the summit overlooks An Garbh Choire, above which sits a series of magnificent hanging corries: Coire Bhrochain, Garbh Choire Dhàidh and Garbh Choire Mòr on Braeriach; together with Corrie of the Chokestone Gully and Coire an Lochain Uaine on Sgòr an Lochain Uaine and Cairn Toul opposite. It is a great cirque; a massive natural amphitheatre that is a truly wondrous sight. Topped with imposing cliffs, these great bowls can hold snow well into summer and in their innermost recesses even all year. The cornices that form on Braeriach are amongst the biggest and most continuous of any in the country. Braeriach translates from the Gaelic Am Bràigh Riabhach as The Brindled Upland, which may relate to the mottled appearance of the resilient vegetation that exists within what can be an incredibly inhospitable environment.

Braeriach is an awkward mountain to reach, with all the approach options on foot being fairly long. Of these, an approach from the Sugarbowl car park, on the left just before the zigzags on the access road to Cairn Gorm, is

START & FINISH: Sugarbowl Car Park (NH985074); pay & display
DISTANCE: 21km; 13miles
HEIGHT GAIN: 1170m; 3840ft
APPROX TIME: 7hrs 30mins–8hrs 30mins

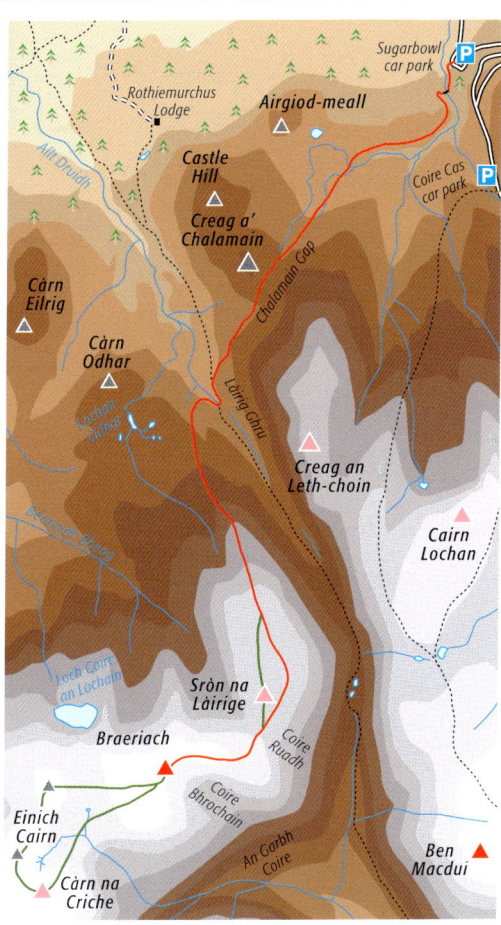

summit. The natural return is by the route of ascent.

Leave the Sugarbowl car park in its upper corner by a link path to the road, which is crossed to descend a woodland path to the Allt Mòr (Great Water) whose crystal clear waters tumble down through the Glenmore Forest Park. Dipper scuttle about the rocks and water throughout the year here, with grey and pied wagtail frequenting the river-bank and woodland during summer.

Cross the wooden bridge (Utsi's Bridge, named after the Reindeer herder, see p83) that spans the river and take the path which climbs up right out of the beautiful wooded gorge, turning left at the top. A gradual climb south then south-west on a well-constructed path leads above the upper reaches of the gorge, along what is known as a kame terrace.

probably the best. Traversing across the lower slopes of Cairn Gorm then passing through the Chalamain Gap, this route crosses the great through pass of the Làirig Ghru to climb the ridge of Sròn na Làirige to gain the

This glacial feature marks the position of the Glen More ice sheet where melt-water ponded against it; see **Stac na h-Iolaire** [6].

The view across to **Cairn Gorm & Northern Corries** [7] is superb, whilst

Braeriach from the Sugarbowl

Creag an Leth-choin and the Chalamain Gap

ahead, between Creag an Leth-choin and Creag a' Chalamain, lies the distinctive notch of the Chalamain Gap with the smaller notch of the Eag a' Chait further right; both glacial meltwater channels.

Descend to cross the small burn of the Caochan Dubh a' Chadha, then make a steady ascent towards the deep fissure of the Chalamain Gap, re-crossing the burn a few times. Initially a clear path climbs into the gap but it soon peters out and a jumble of boulders now stands in the way. Progress is slowed when heading over the boulders but with care they should present no real issues. There are times in winter when the gap could become a potential

Chalamain Gap with Meall a' Bhuachaille beyond

Braeriach from the Sugarbowl

Approaching the Làirig Ghru with Braeriach and Sgòr Gaoith ahead

avalanche trap and it may be better to take a route across the side of, or over, Creag a' Chalamain to the right.

On the other side of the gap, the well-constructed path continues and the landscape opens with spacious views ahead to Braeriach's hulking outline and across to Sgòr Gaoith [21]. Easy walking now leads downhill across the flanks of Creag an Leth-choin into the Làirig Ghru where a final steep descent leads to the floor of one of the most famous mountain passes in Scotland.

Thought to mean Gloomy Pass, the Làirig Ghru was, for centuries, the main link through the Cairngorms between Speyside and Deeside and was later used by drovers and cattle thieves to herd cattle through. Due to its elevation of 833m at its highest point, and the wild weather and snow that affected the route throughout the year, calves were driven along the lower Làirig an Laoigh to the east (see p36). Such was the importance of the Làirig Ghru to the local economy that men were sent up every spring to clear the paths of boulders left after the winter.

Turn left along the path coming up from Rothiemurchus used by Càrn Eilrig [17] and walk beside the waters of the Allt Druidh for 100m or so (passing the Sinclair memorial) to where the river emerges from beneath a boulder field. Flat boulders here provide an amazing and convenient crossing point. On the other side, another well-engineered path leaves the path through the làirig to climb steeply up the other side to a flattening (the site of the former Sinclair Memorial Hut, see p105), then continue up to the ridge leading onto the northern shoulder of Sròn na Làirige (Nose of the Pass).

The initial section of this ridge is quite sustained, but when the angle eases at

Allt Druidh crossing

Braeriach from the Sugarbowl

Cairn Toul and Sgòr an Lochain Uaine

the first of a few small boulder fields, take the path up left along the crest to make the most of the impressive views down into and across the Làirig Ghru to Creag an Leth-choin (Lurcher's Crag) and Ben Macdui.

Higher, the ridge broadens and the gradient eases completely with the path crossing easy grassy terrain. At a clear fork, go right and rise slightly to pass left of and just below the actual top of Sròn na Làirige (1184m), a subsidiary Munro Top (see p5) that can be taken in on the way up, or down, if desired.

Dotterel

Scotland holds all of Britain's breeding population of this rare bird and they have a specially protected status. In migration they fly in groups know as trips. Nesting begins during May and takes place above 1000m, in amongst scrapes of moss and lichen that are prevalent on the high ground of the Cairngorms. Identifable by their brief undulating piping call and their markings, a chestnut-coloured breast and white streak above the eye, they are unusual in that the females are the more colourful. They are one of a few species where the male does practically all the incubating and rearing whilst the female goes off to mate again. They are easily confused with the similar Golden Plover (p105).

Braeriach from the Sugarbowl

Cairn Lochan and the Làirig Ghru from Sròn na Làirige

Beyond this, the path drops to a broad col between Coire Ruadh on the làirig side and Coire Beanaidh on the right. Scattered about here are the remnants of an RAF Oxford which crashed in October 1943 and a Bristol Blenheim which crashed in March 1945.

A final steep ascent up the gravelly slope ahead gains the edge of Coire Bhrochain, where a delightful walk up and around the rim leads to the summit cairn (1296m), which lies a few metres back from the cliff edge.

The panorama is jaw dropping; Ben Macdui's sprawling mass sits across the Làirig Ghru from the entrance to An Garbh Coire, whilst the next two highest mountains after Ben Macdui and Braeriach lie on the far side of this great amphitheatre; the shapely Cairn Toul and Sgòr an Lochain Uaine (The Angel's Peak), with the lovely Lochan Uaine nestling in the corrie below.

To return, retrace your steps to the Làirig Ghru then through the Chalamain Gap back to the Sugarbowl.

Einich Cairn extension
The plateau extends westwards from Braeriach's summit and it is worth walking south-west across this to Einich Cairn (1237m) to admire the view across the great glacial trough holding Loch Eanaich to Sgòr Gaoith, before seeking out the source of the River Dee at the Wells of Dee. Càrn na Criche (1265m), the outlying south-western Munro Top of Braeriach, lies a little south of the wells, above the head of Garbh Choire Mòr, and is easily included. From there, Sgòr an Lochain Uaine (The Angel's Peak) and Cairn Toul lie temptingly close and, together with the Devil's Point, could be included for a complete circuit of An Garbh Choire with a return from Corrour bothy past the Pools of Dee and the highest point of the Làirig Ghru. This is a mammoth outing which some take two days over. However, for the route described here, simply return to the summit of Braeriach around the bowl of Garbh Choire Dhàidh, past the edge where the water runs over to form the Falls of Dee. A scenic there and back trip adding 5km, 120m of height gain and 1hr 30mins to the main route.

15 Braeriach from Whitewell
Britain's third highest mountain

Braeriach's summit with Ben Macdui beyond and distant Lochnagar

Braeriach's distance from the nearest road means it is not an easy mountain to reach and all the approaches to it are long. That being said, each route onto the summit of Britain's third highest mountain is a stunning experience. Braeriach from the Sugarbowl [14] describes the approach from the access road to Cairn Gorm, which is probably the most popular. However, a circuit from Whitewell (or Coylumbridge) via the long, lonely and wild confines of Gleann Eanaich with a return to the Làirig Ghru and through the Rothiemurchus forest, is perhaps the finest.

Start from a small car park at Whitewell, at the end of the unclassified minor road that leaves the Cairn Gorm access road at Inverdruie between Aviemore and Coylumbridge. Coming from Aviemore this is 300m beyond the B970 turn-off for Inshriach and Loch an Eilein and it is signed to Tullochgrue and Black Park. There is additional verge parking just before the car park.

Leave the north end of the car park by a path on the right through the bushes and cross a small bridge to gain the main track from Coylumbridge, then continue south along this.

Although it is some 4km longer overall, a start can also be made along this track, from a layby on the right side of the road some 350m past the entrance to the Coylumbridge Hotel. This is beside the entrance to the Rothiemurchus Camp & Caravan Park.

START & FINISH: Whitewell car park (NH915086)
DISTANCE: 26.5km; 16.5 miles
HEIGHT GAIN: 1080m; 3550ft
APPROX TIME: 8hrs 30mins–9hrs 30mins

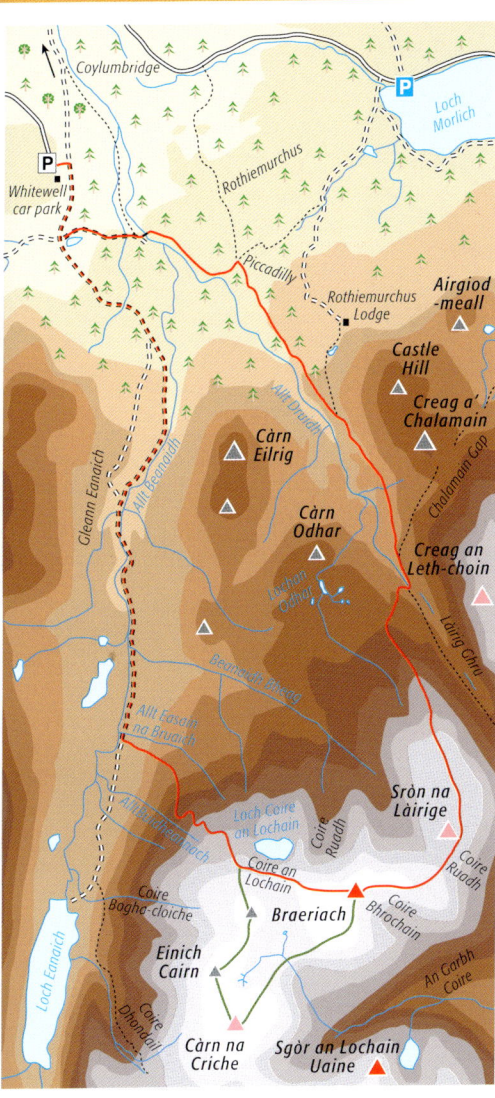

The track runs to the right of this into the woodland of Rothiemurchus. After about 650m, keep right at a fork for Glen Eanaich and continue for a further 1.35km to where the route from Whitewell joins the track.

Pass through two gates and at a crossroads at Lochan Deò (Little Loch of the Sparkling), continue straight ahead on a track that veers southeast with views past Càrn Eilrig [17] to Braeriach.

When the track splits, keep to the lower one which runs alongside the rapid flow coming out of Gleann Eanaich. This is the Am Beanaidh and its banks are bounded by fine specimens of Scots pine and rowan with the slopes of Càrn Eilrig rising steeply on the left. The glen is particularly impressive during autumn, when the russets and browns of the vegetation and the bright red rowan berries are striking.

Soon the trees are left behind and a footbridge over the Am

Braeriach from Whitewell

Càrn Eilrig above the Am Beanaidh

Beanaidh is crossed. Rising slopes on either side give the glen a remote air and the enormous flanks of Braeriach dominate the view. Continue along the river's eastern bank and cross the Beanaidh Bheag via stepping stones, or a wade; in spate it may be impassable.

In another 1km, and 2.25km short of Loch Eanaich, just after crossing the Allt Easan na Bruiach, bear left from the track onto the huge north-western slopes of Braeriach.

The next section is the toughest of the walk, with steep and generally pathless ground leading to the extensive summit of Braeriach. In poor weather good navigation may be called on. Initially a slightly marshy section leads onto drier ground from where a rising ascent south-east, away from the Allt Easan na Bruaich, leads up steepening grassy slopes. An old stalkers' path starts just above the 700m contour and zigzags up the hillside over by the Allt Bhuidheannach. If found it may aid progress, but it disappears below the level of the corrie and may be more trouble to locate than it is worth. Mountain hare, snow bunting and golden eagle may well be seen on this little-frequented part of Braeriach. As height is gained there are superb views of Loch Eanaich and the cliffs of **Sgòr Gaoith** [21] and Sgòran Dubh Mòr.

Am Beanaidh

Braeriach from Whitewell

Braeriach's summit and Coire Bhrochain

The gradient relents briefly to the west of the beautiful Loch Coire an Lochain, which sits in a bowl at the base of Coire an Lochain, before the ascent continues up the slope ahead. Higher, follow the natural line east above the cliff edge towards north facing Coire Ruadh, before making the final short climb south-east to gain Braeriach's 1296m summit. The cairn sits perched almost on the very edge of the cliffs overlooking Coire Bhrochain. It is a fabulous viewpoint, with much of the national park laid out before you. To the south, on the other side of the great cirque of An Garbh Choire, Cairn Toul and Sgòr an Lochain Uaine (the Angel's Peak) in particular catch the eye, with Ben Macdui sitting opposite on the other side of the Làirig Ghru.

Leave the summit by following the edge of Coire Bhrochain north-east, then east down gravelly slopes to a dip before a slight rise. From there, descend the open gravelly slope to a col between Coire Beanaidh on the left and south-east facing Coire Ruadh on the right. Scattered about here are the remains of an RAF Oxford which crashed in October 1943 and a Bristol Blenheim which crashed in March 1945.

Einich Cairn Extension
On the ascent to the summit plateau of Braeriach, a diversion southwards, away from the route up the side of Coire an Lochain, gains the fine viewpoint of Einich Cairn (137m). From there, head south past the Wells of Dee (the source of the River Dee) and make the short ascent onto Càrn na Criche (1265m) above Garbh Choire Mòr at the head of the great An Garbh Choire cirque. This is one of Braeraich's two outlying Munro Tops; the other being Sròn na Làirige which is on the route down. Head northwards around the edge of Garbh Choire Dhàidh, past where the burn drops over the edge to form the Falls of Dee, and ascend to the top of Braeriach; this adds 3.5km, 90m of ascent and 50min to the main route.

Braeriach from Whitewell

Aircraft wreckage on the eastern slopes of Braeriach. Sròn na Làirige above and Cairn Lochan on the right

From the col, the path rises up the slope ahead to pass just below the featureless summit of Sròn na Làirige (1184m), one of Braeriach's two subsidiary Munro Tops (see p5), which can easily be included by a slight diversion. The view across the Làirig Ghru to Creag an Leth-choin is splendid. The path becomes a little hard to follow where it passes through some boulder fields, then improves as it drops more steeply down the end of the long northern shoulder of Sròn na Làirige.

At the bottom, continue easily north-east towards the distinctive summit of Creag a' Chalamain on the opposite side of the Làirig Ghru. Pass a flattening

Descending to the Làirig Ghru with Creag a' Chalamain ahead

Braeriach from Whitewell

near the edge, the site of the former Sinclar hut, then drop steeply to the floor of the Làirig Ghru.

Cross the Allt Druidh on boulders where it emerges from a blockage and follow the path north, passing the Sinclair memorial plaque on a boulder, then the path that breaks off up right to the Chalamain Gap, taken by Braeriach from the Sugarbowl [14] and Creag a' Chalamain [16]. The path now descends gently across open moorland, although its rough underfoot in places, then passes through a small flat-floored valley to the side of a moraine mound, before dropping into the lovely wooded confines of Rothiemurchus, and passing a path off right to Rothiemurchus Lodge.

Continue to a crossroads of paths, known as Piccadilly, and turn left, keeping on through the woodland. The path soon swings right to run alongside the Allt Druidh then its confluence with the Am Beanaidh, which is eventually crossed by the wonderful iron Cairngorm Club Footbridge that dates from 1912.

If returning to the road at Coylumbridge, bear right at a fork after 150m and follow the path then track back. Otherwise, continue ahead on the track to regain the crossroads at Lochan Deò and turn right back to Whitewell, keeping an eye out for the small bridge on the left after the second gate.

Golden Plover

Throughout the winter months these birds will invariably be found at lower levels, usually in flocks and often with lapwings.

However, during the summer, resplendent in their attractive black and gold feathers (buff and white during winter) they are more solitary and happily reside on the higher plateau and mountain tops of the Cairngorms.

Watch where you place your feet as the little feathery ball of a golden plover chick may be found wandering, not far from their ground nests. They can be confused with the similar dotterel (see p98), however the golden plover is slightly larger, has a distinctive plaintive call and a characteristic running or flitting about from mound to mound, or boulder to boulder, which can make them hard to locate in the flat terrain.

They are generally spotted away from where they made the call, briefly standing still and upright.

105

16 Creag a' Chalamain
A fine low-level circuit of Cairn Gorm's foothills

Although this route doesn't venture onto the high tops of the Cairngorms, it still climbs to a height of 787m and should not be taken lightly. Beginning from Loch Morlich the route travels through the Rothiemurchus forest to the Làirig Ghru, then up to the Chalamain Gap to ascend Creag a' Chalamain and neighbouring Airgiod-meall, before returning through the Glenmore Forest Park.

Loch Morlich has several car parks situated along its northern shore and this walk utilises the one at its north-western edge; some 3 miles (5km) east of Coylumbridge. This is on the edge of what is known as The Queen's Forest, which extends north up the flanks of the Kincardineshire Hills; a memorial in the trees on the north side of the road from the car park commemorates the naming for Queen Mary during the 1935 Silver Jubilee of King George V.

Walk west through the trees on a path leading to the road and turn left along the verge for 50m to cross the bridge over the outflow from the loch; the River Luineag. A wide track leads south into the woodland of Rothiemurchus, with views through the trees to the loch. Keep straight on at a fork, signed for the Làirig Ghru, and continue alongside a large area that has been felled on the right, passing lovely Lochan nan Geadas in the trees on the left. Pass a

START & FINISH: Loch Morlich car park (NN958097); pay & display
DISTANCE: 21km; 13 miles
HEIGHT GAIN: 575m; 1890ft
APPROX TIME: 6–7hrs

Creag a' Chalamain from the Làirig Ghru

track off left and carry on to another fork then go right, again signed to the Làirig Ghru. Views to the hills have been opened up here due to felling on the left.

Now on a wide path, progress easily south-west through lovely Caledonian Pine woodland for another 1.4km to a crossroads known as Piccadilly. Take the narrow path on the left which disappears into the forest; signed to the Làirig Ghru. The shaded woodland floor is an ideal habitat for Blaeberry and Cowberry and an eye should be kept out for the amazing ant nests that the forest contains.

The path rises gradually uphill, high above the fast flowing Allt Druidh, its steep banks lined with beautiful stands of birch and Scots pine. Braeriach from Whitewell [15] returns this way from the summit of Braeriach and on the other side of the Allt Druidh gorge,

Creag a' Chalamain

Creag a' Chalamain

Rothiemurchus forest with Ord Bàn and distant Geal-chàrn Mòr

Glenmore & Rothiemurchus Forests
These neighbouring forests are remnants of the ancient Caledonian Forest and they provide a vital ecosystem for a variety of fauna and flora, including, red squirrel, pine marten, crossbill, crested tit, woodpecker, dipper, wood ant, the rare pine hoverfly, creeping lady's tresses and twinflower. Glenmore, simply meaning Big Glen, lies between the lower slopes of Meall a' Bhuachaille and Cairn Gorm and has a unique mixture of woodland, high mountains, rivers and lochs.
Rothiemurchus (Ràt Murchais) means Fort of Murchas with the first people settling here thought to be The Picts, around the 8th century. The estate, covers an area of around 30 square kilometres and has been owned by the Grants of Rothiemurchus since 1567, who today care for one of the largest surviving areas of ancient woodland in Europe, which includes aspen, birch, rowan, willow, juniper and Scots pine.

Càrn Eilrig [17] presents a fine sight. In due course the path climbs away from the woodland onto the open hillside, where it is joined by a path from Rothiemurchus Lodge. The view ahead extends to the cliffs of Creag an Leth-choin (better known as Lurcher's Crag, see p79) on the left and the long spur of Sròn na Làirige leading to Braeriach on the right. In between, the Làirig Ghru, one of the most famous mountain passes in Scotland, slices deeply through the heart of the Northern Cairngorms.

The path becomes rougher underfoot across flat ground for a way, before a section of improved path leads to, then alongside the early stages of the Allt Druidh, which tumbles out of a narrow, steep-sided channel. The onward route ascends another path out of this channel, but first it is worth continuing for 100m or so (passing the Sinclair memorial plaque, see p105) to view the Allt Druidh emerging from beneath a boulder field blockage. This provides the crossing point for routes through the Làirig Ghru and onto Braeriach.

Creag a' Chalamain

Braeriach from Creag 'a Chalamain

Return to ascend the well-constructed stepped path that rises up the steep side of the channel to gain easier-angled ground. Now heading towards the Chalamain Gap, the path climbs steadily up the lower slopes of Creag an Leth-choin with pointed Creag a' Chalamain rising ahead.

The Chalamain Gap is a craggy, steep-sided, boulder-filled glacial meltwater channel, which is worth viewing; in the distance Ben Rinnes is nicely framed by its sides. The gap provides the principal through route to the Làirig Ghru from Cairn Gorm; Braeriach from the Sugarbowl [14] travels through the gap on its way to and from the summit. About 100m before the gap, break off left up another path to make the short, but steep climb onto Creag a' Chalamain (787m). Its Gaelic translation is thought to mean Crag of the Corrie of the Assembly and its rocky summit provides a splendid viewpoint.

Kincardineshire Hills & Loch Morlich from Creag a' Chalamain

Creag a' Chalamain

Cairn Gorm & The Northern Corries over Lochan Dubh a' Chadha, Airgiod-meall

Braeriach and its northern corries stand out, as does Càrn Eilrig with Sgòr Gaoith beyond, Rothiemurchus, Glen More and the Kincardineshire Hills.

Drop north-west to a shallow saddle, then go up the slight rise onto the flat top of Castle Hill (728m), before descending north-east towards the left side of a ravine below. This is the Eag a' Chait (Notch of the Cat), another melt-water channel similar to, but not as impressive as the Chalamain Gap. Cross over past the entrance to the gap to a gate in the fence (the reindeer enclosure); the gate does not open, but it is easy to take your rucksack off and step through between the upper and lower parts of the fence.

Ascend onto the rounded top of Airgiod-meall (644m), which is a superb spot from which to appreciate Cairn Gorm and its two Northern Corries (Coire an t-Sneachda and Coire an Lochain), together with the splendid outlook over the Glenmore Forest to Loch Morlich and the **Kincardineshire Hills** [1].

Descend south-east to a path beside small Lochan Dubh a' Chadha and follow this south to a stile and gate to

Meall a' Bhuachaille and Kincardineshire Hills

Creag a' Chalamain

exit the enclosure. Continue alongside the fence on the flat ground of a glacial feature known as a kame terrace, which indicates a level of the Glen More ice sheet (see **Stac na h-Iolaire [6]**) during the Ice Age. At some point, cross to the right to meet the main path coming down from the Chalamain Gap after it has crossed the dip of the Chaochan Dubh a' Chadha burn. The path swings round and descends beside the fenced enclosure, then cuts back right to drop into the Allt Mòr gorge and cross the river by Utsi's bridge (see p83). Turn left along the Allt Mòr Trail and follow this through lovely woodland by the river for 1km to reach the road.

Utsi's Bridge

Cross over and continue on the trail through the Glenmore woodland to reach a track, then turn left across a bridge over the Allt Mòr into the Allt Mòr car park. Go down the left side on a path to cross the access track and continue through woodland. When the path splits, keep right and follow it to reach the road where the river passes beneath a bridge. This is now the Abhainn Ruigh-eunachan, which the Allt Mòr has joined. Cross the bridge to gain the entrance to the Allt Bàn car park.

The quickest way back is to follow the roadside verge past the Glenmore Visitor Centre car park to pick up the Old Logging Way on the north side of the road. This track is followed for a final 1.75km to opposite the entrance to the car park at the start.

A pleasant and slightly longer alternative is to cross the road opposite the Allt Bàn car park and follow the riverside path for 1km to beyond a bridge, then gain the beach at the head of Loch Morlich; Scotland's only freshwater award-winning beach. The rough sands are composed of coarse granite, ground down by nature and the elements. Walk the sands to reach the Boathouse (cafe & toilets), beyond which the road can be crossed in a few places to gain the Old Logging Way.

Loch Morlich

Càrn Eilrig from the Làirig Ghru path above the Allt Druidh

17 Càrn Eilrig
An isolated and less frequented peak

Càrn Eilrig from Càrn Odhar

Càrn Eilrig is the shapely pointed hill that features prominently in the view from the north when looking towards the Cairngorm massif. It sits out in front of Braeriach, between the entrances to the Làirig Ghru and Gleann Eanaich, and is an awkward hill to approach since the rivers that flow out of these glens practically form a moat around it. A further barrier to a direct approach from the north is given by the Rothiemurchus forest. This isolated position, together with its lowly height, when compared to its neighbours, means that Càrn Eilrig is rarely ascended.

For anyone prepared to venture off the beaten track though, the walk to attain its summit, which is a fabulous viewpoint, gives a superb and varied outing. An approach is made via the Làirig Ghru to ascend Càrn Eilrig and its neighbour, Càrn Odhar, by a surprisingly easy back door route from the south, with a return via Gleann Eanaich.

Start from a small car park at Whitewell, at the end of the unclassified minor road that leaves the Cairn Gorm access road at Inverdruie between Aviemore and Coylumbridge. Coming from Aviemore this is 300m beyond the B970 turn-off for Inshriach and Loch an Eilein and it is signed to Tullochgrue and Black Park. There is additional verge parking just before the car park.

Leave the north end of the car park by a path on the right through the bushes and cross a small bridge to gain the main track from Coylumbridge. Turn right along the track through lovely woodland, passing through two gates to reach a crossroads. Go left, signed to the Làirig Ghru, past little Lochan Deò and in a further 1.5km cross the Cairngorm Club Footbridge over the Am Beanaidh; just before the bridge there is a stone memorial in the trees on the

START & FINISH: Whitewell car park (NH915086)
DISTANCE: 22km; 13.5 miles
HEIGHT GAIN: 655m; 2150ft
APPROX TIME: 6hrs 30mins–7hrs 30mins

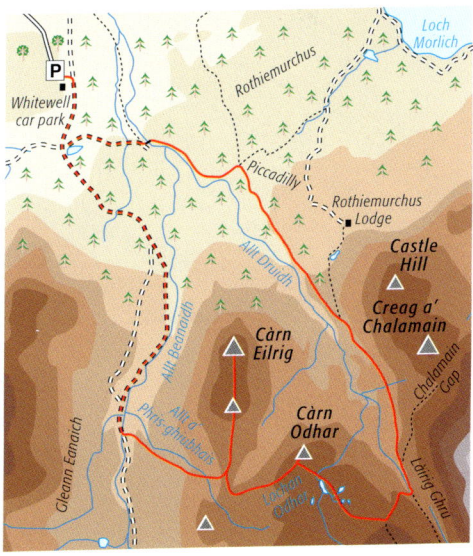

left. Pass the confluence of the Am Beanaidh, which flows out of Gleann Eanaich, and the Allt Druid, which flows out of the Làirig Ghru, and continue through an open area before swinging left, back into the trees, to reach a path junction known as Piccadilly. The route to Creag a' Chalamain [16] arrives here from Loch Morlich and travels the same way for the next 4.5km.

Take the narrow path on the right, signed to the Làirig Ghru, and disappear into the forest, climbing gradually uphill high above the Allt Druidh through beautiful woodland full of bird song. Higher, as the trees thin out and become smaller, there are fine views across the gorge to Càrn Eilrig; the route Braeriach from Whitewell [15] returns this way.

At the upper limit of the trees, the path from Rothiemurchus Lodge joins in from the left and the path continues gently uphill towards the cliffs of Creag an Leth-choin (better known as Lurcher's Crag – see p79), which line the left side of the Làirig Ghru pass ahead.

The path becomes rougher underfoot across flat ground for a way, before a section of improved path leads to, then alongside the Allt Druidh, which tumbles out of a narrow, steep-sided channel. Continue into this narrowing channel past the path up left to Creag a' Chalamain and the Chalamain Gap, then the Sinclair memorial (see p105), and cross the Allt Druidh on flat boulders where it emerges from beneath a boulder field blockage; an interesting spectacle. On the other side, leave the Làirig Ghru path and ascend steeply up right via the well-engineered path to Braeriach to arrive at a flattening; the site of the former Sinclair Memorial Hut.

Continue uphill with splendid views of Creag an Leth-choin and the Làirig Ghru to reach a small channel where the path to Braeriach starts the steeper climb onto the Sròn na Làirige ridge. Instead, follow a rough, grassy path through to the far side of the channel, to where Sgòran Dubh Mòr and Sgòr Gaoith come into view. Leave the path here and find a slightly raised line that gives easy walking downhill to the north-west, across a broad plateau. Pass to the left of some small lochans

115

Càrn Eilrig

Creag an Leth-choin and the Làirig Ghru from Càrn Odhar

to reach the splendidly situated Lochan Odhar with its lovely granitic sands and cross the outflow just before the burn starts to drop downhill. A short ascent leads onto the top of Càrn Odhar (734m) where the cairn sits at the north-east end overlooking the Làirig Ghru; a good spot for a lunch stop. Creag a' Chalamain sits on the opposite side of the Làirig Ghru and from here its shape looks remarkably like Càrn Eilrig to the north.

Return along the crest and take a line which makes a short descent to curve around the high ground, then drop to a narrow boulder-filled meltwater channel at a height of 629m. A rough path is picked up here and followed uphill on ground that gives further easy walking to gain the south top of Càrn Eilrig (722m), then after crossing the dip, the cairned summit (742m). Backed by the immense bulk of Braeriach, the isolated position in the narrowing of the jaws between Gleann Eanaich and the Làirig Ghru means it is a fabulous viewpoint. Creag Dubh [18] lies to the west whilst Creag a' Chalamain is to the east. To

Creag a' Chalamain from Càrn Odhar

Càrn Eilrig

Approaching the summit of Càrn Eilrig

the north the ground falls away steeply and there is a commanding view out across the vastness of the Rothiemurchus forest, with Loch Morlich and the **Kincardineshire Hills** [1] beyond.

The aim now is to gain the bridge which can be seen crossing the Am Beanaidh in Gleann Eanaich at NH924042. To do so, return to the 629m col, then descend diagonally across the hillside to reach the Allt a' Phris-ghiubhais, which is followed a short way before crossing it. Cross the flat ground below, go up a slight rise then through some haggy ground on the flat top and drop to the track to reach the bridge.

Follow the lower track back into the Rothiemurchus forest, joined by the route off Creag Dubh, and continue for just over 4km to go through a gate. Continue ahead past Lochan Deò (left leads to Loch an Eilein) to the track crossroads encountered at the start of the day, then back to Whitewell, keeping an eye out for the small bridge on the left after the second gate.

Braeriach from Càrn Eilrig

117

18 Creag Dhubh
Loch an Eilein & The Argyll Stone

Creag Dhubh across Loch an Eilein

When compared to its bigger neighbours, Creag Dhubh is a smaller and more compact mountain, with its broad summit ridge only rising to 848m. However, it is a hill that should not be underestimated, for the ascent is much rougher and tougher than many of its neighbours. It does give a rewarding walk though, and the views from its summit ridge are superb. Beginning from the tranquil setting of Loch an Eilein, the western flanks of Creag Dhubh are traversed to ascend Coire Follais to reach Clach Mhic Cailein (The Argyll Stone) then the summit itself. A scenic return is made by Gleann Eanaich.

There is a car park at the north end of Loch an Eilein, below the wooded slopes of Ord Bàn. It is accessed from the roundabout at the south end of Aviemore by leaving the road to Cairn Gorm and turning right after 1km at Inverdruie, then left after 1.7km along a short unclassified road.

Leave the car park and follow a path south to the loch, where there is a fine view of Creag Dhubh; to the right is a visitor centre with gallery, shop, cafe and toilets. Loch an Eilein means Loch of the Island, the island in it being famous for its castle; see p125 **Ord Ban & Kennapole Hill** [19] which also walks around the loch as well as climbing the two small hills that overlook it.

Although paths around either side of the loch can be taken, the path around the right (west) side is shorter and, as well as affording good views over the loch to Creag Dhubh, it passes the island with its castle. There are also some fine examples of Scots pine trees on the way. Swing around the far side of the loch and continue south-east to cross a bridge over the outflow from Loch Gamhna, then turn off right along

START & FINISH: Loch an Eilein car park (NH897085), parking charge
DISTANCE: 18km; 11 miles
HEIGHT GAIN: 600m; 1970ft
APPROX TIME: 5hrs 30mins–6hrs 30mins

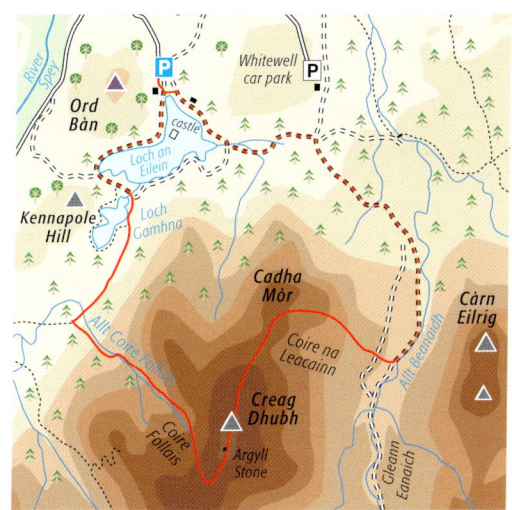

a narrow path above the east side of that loch.

Keep to the left after 300m, passing through more lovely woodland to enter the Invereshie & Inshriach National Nature Reserve. After another 1.25km cross the Allt Coire Follais which is normally straightforward. In a further 150m, and just before some large Scots pines, take a narrow path which cuts back sharply left; maps show the path starting from the bothy a little further on, but that path has disappeared and is not now the route on the ground.

The path becomes a little overgrown and rough underfoot (although it's always clear) as it climbs quite steeply south-east through heather. As height is gained, views open out north over Loch Gamhna to Kennapole Hill. Soon the

119

Creag Dhubh

Braeriach, Gleann Eanaich and Sgòran Dubh Mòr from Creag Dhubh

path, flanked with blaeberry, bog cotton and common spotted orchid, runs alongside the Allt Coire Follais, which is crossed higher up; normally easy on stepping stones.

Keep on up the north bank of the burn, eventually rising above the treeline. At the head of a ravine, where the burn peters out, it is possible to leave the path and climb directly to The Argyll Stone, which can be seen standing prominently on the skyline ridge above. However, it is better to keep to the now vague path and traverse gradually uphill to the south for almost 700m onto the right-hand shoulder.

On meeting a path coming up from Creag Follais, follow this left onto the crest of the ridge to be met by a fabulous view. South along the linking ridge is Sgòran Dubh Mòr, climbed on the ascent of **Sgòr Gaoith** [21], whilst west across the Spey valley lie the Monadh Liath Mountains. Eastwards is **Càrn Eilrig** [17] with Creag an Leth-choin, Cairn Gorm and the Northern Corries

---

Ring Ouzel
Similar in colour to the blackbird, but slightly smaller and slimmer, the ring ouzell is conspicuous by its white bib, or collar. Although, with only around 5000 breeding pairs left in Scotland they are much scarcer than their common cousins. The migration of ring ouzel brings them to Scotland from Scandinavia in March/April before they fly off in September for the warmer climes of North Africa. They are fiercely protective of their nest, which is usually found on craggy outcrops, or steep-sided valleys and gullies.

Creag Dhubh

beyond, but it is the impressive sight of Braeriach's massive bulk to the south-east across Gleann Eanaich that really draws the attention, with the ascent route for **Braeriach from Whitewell** [15] visible.

Continue easily along the rocky crest to gain first The Argyll Stone, then the flat summit of Creag Dhubh where the view opens to the north up the Spey valley over Aviemore. Ben Rinnes (below which the Battle of Glenlivet took place, see panel opposite) is visible between **Meall a' Bhuachaille** [2] and Creagan Gorm in the **Kincardineshire Hills** [1].

To descend, head north to a cairn at the northern edge of the ridge, then drop north-east to a shallow saddle, the Cadha Mòr, at the head of a grassy Coire na Leacainn on the right. Rather than go down this, it is better to keep to the high ground with views over Loch an Eilein and Speyside to follow the ridge as it swings round and descends towards Càrn Eilrig into Gleann Eanaich, with a great view into this deep glacial trough, where there are some fine moraines.

Head for a rounded, grassy knoll and once over this, descend to the upper track above the floor of the glen. Either

The Argyll Stone
Sitting close to the flat summit of Creag Dhubh is one of many granite tors in the Cairngorm National Park that have been eroded and shaped by the weather over many millennia. Rising to about 4m in height, The Argyll Stone (Clach Mhic Cailein) is thought to have been named after Archibald Campbell, the 7th Earl of Argyll. In 1594, Campbell's Protestant army was defeated by the much smaller Catholic force of the Marquis of Huntly at the Battle of Glenlivet, which took place in the foothills to the south of Ben Rinnes. After this, the Earl and his men fled through the Cairngorms, reputedly pausing at Clach Mhic Cailein before continuing their retreat.

turn left along this or, better, drop to the lower track just above the Am Beanaidh and follow the river through lovely woodland; both tracks join 2km further on at a small burn. In another 1.75km, pass through a gate beside Lochan Deò, then go left and left again after a few metres, then left again after 100m. Continue for 1km to reach the track around Loch an Eilein and turn right along this back to the car park.

19 Kennapole Hill & Ord Bàn
Tranquil Loch an Eilein & two small hills

Kennapole Hill, Ord Bàn, Loch Gamhna and Loch an Eilein

This lovely short walk on the edge of the Rothiemurchus forest makes a circuit of tranquil Loch an Eilein and neighbouring Loch Gamhna, as well as climbing two of The Cairngorms minor foothills; Kennapole Hill (385m) and Ord Bàn (428m). The walk is best undertaken as a clockwise circuit since this offers the optimum lighting conditions for viewing the beautiful surroundings. For this reason it is also best to ascend Ord Bàn, whose summit is a superb viewpoint, at the end of the walk. Start from the car park at the north end of Loch an Eilein, at the foot of the wooded slopes of Ord Bàn. The car park is accessed from the roundabout at the south end of Aviemore by leaving the road to Cairn Gorm and turning right at Inverdruie after 1km, then left after 1.7km along a short unclassified road.

Leave the car park and follow a path south to the loch, passing the visitor centre with gallery, shop, cafe and toilets. Loch an Eilein means Loch of the Island, the island in it being famous for its castle, which can be seen with the wooded slopes beyond rising to Creag Dhubh [18]. Cross the outflow by a footbridge and follow the track into the forest passing Forest Cottage. All the way along this section, it is worth

Loch Gamhna and Kennapole Hill

START & FINISH: Loch an Eilein car park (NH897085), parking charge
DISTANCE: 10.5km; 6.5 miles
HEIGHT GAIN: 330m
APPROX TIME: 3–4hrs

diverting from the track to follow some of the many paths that lead down to the waters edge for the view across the loch. Pass the track off left to the Làirig Ghru and Gleann Eanaich and continue along the south side of the loch.

Shortly after crossing a small footbridge, take a path off to the left at a 'Path not maintained' sign and follow this through the trees above Loch Gamhna; loch of the stirks (young) cattle. Turn right after 300m and follow a narrow path down towards the loch then swing round across boggy ground at its head. On the far side, turn off left along another path which runs through a gap in a drystane wall after 100m. It is possible to follow the path to a track that joins the main forest track then turn right up this to reach a crossroad where a right turn regains the wall on the crest. However, this is 2km longer than simply following rough ground uphill beside the wall, probably easiest on the left side, to meet the path coming from the track on the left. Go through a gap in the wall and climb onto the wooded top of Kennapole Hill with its large Duchess of Bedford's Cairn erected for Georgiana Russell (formerly Lady Georgiana Gordon), see p128 and panel on p149. The inscription dated 1834 reads:

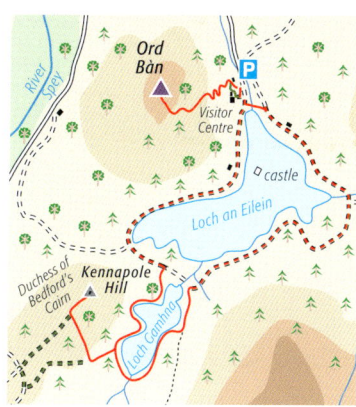

To her whose eye explored and whose steps marked with discriminating taste this little path from Loch Gaun to the Cats Den and round the craig of Kinapole to its summit this simple tablet is inscribed by a sincere and affectionate friend
A.D. MDCCCXXXIV Bedford

There is a stunning view over Loch an Eilein and Rothiemurchus to **Meall a' Bhuachaille** [2] and the **Kincardineshire Hills** [1]. After taking time to enjoy this lovely spot, return to Loch Gamhna and follow the path along its north-west side to rejoin the main path around Loch an Eilein. At a bench, either cut the corner, or continue to the junction then go right, and follow the track along the north side of the loch. There are some splendid pine trees on this section. Go

Kennapole Hill & Ord Bàn

Loch an Eilein from Kennapole Hill

through a gate to reach Loch an Eilein Cottage, then leave the track and go down a path to the waters edge to view the castle on the island with Cairn Gorm rising beyond. From here, it is only a short distance back to the car park.

For starting the ascent to Ord Bàn there two options. The first is to go to the small building in the north corner of the car park and climb a vertical ladder stile to the side of a gate, then go left on a path that slants up the slope. The other is to cross the fence to the side of the toilet block by an angled ladder stile, then follow the fence rightwards for 200m until almost opposite the small building to pick up the path. Either way, the path zigzags up the hillside through lovely woodland, beside a

Rothiemurchus and Cairn Gorm from Ord Bàn

Kennapole Hill & Ord Bàn

wall for a way, before popping out onto the shoulder and climbing across some glacially buffed slabs to reach the trig pillar with adjacent erratic boulder that adorn the summit. Ord Bàn, Kennapole Hill and Torr Alvie [20] with its Duke of Gordon's Monument, which can be seen opposite in the middle of the Spey Valley, are effectively large scale examples of roche moutonnee (see p43) created and left behind by the glacier that flowed down the valley during the ice age.

The 360 degree panorama is superb and it is with some difficulty that one has to leave this splendid spot. Although a path heads west, then south off the summit, this soon peters out, with rough and awkward ground having to be crossed to gain Loch an Eilein at its western end. So, other than going a short way along this to take in the view over the River Spey, it is best to return by the route of ascent.

Loch an Eilein Castle
This ruined castle has a long and mixed history. The lands of Rothiemurchus (Ràt Murchais, the fort of Murchas) were royally granted to the Bishop of Moray in 1226, whom it would appear built on the island.

In 1370, the Earl of Buchan, Alexander Stuart, (Robert the Bruce's grandson), also known as the Wolf of Badenoch, became the protector of the current Bishop and the lands of Rothiemurchus, and it would appear he built more defensively on the island. This relationship failed and resulted in Stuart sacking and burning Forres and Elgin in 1390. Rothiemurchus has been under the care of the Grant family since around 1567; John Grant being designated 'of Rothiemurchus' by King James VI. In the 1600s Patrick Grant of Rothiemurchus also built on the island and in 1690 it was successfully defended by old folk, women and children, from Jacobites who attacked it on their retreat after the Battle of Cromdale. In 1746, Jean Gordon (Grizel Mhòr) widow of James Grant the 5th Laird of Grant would appear to have sheltered fleeing Jacobites there after the Battle of Culloden. Following the raising of the loch to float timber to the Spey around 1770, the castle fell into disrepair.

20 Torr Alvie
A short and scenic walk through beautiful woodland

Spey Valley from Torr Alvie

Located in the middle of the Spey Valley, a short distance to the south of Aviemore, this small wooded hill provides a lovely short walk through beautiful woodland to view the Waterloo Cairn and Duke of Gordon's Monument. The views of the Spey Valley and the surrounding hills are splendid and it is a walk that can be equally appreciated at any time of day.

Start from the Dalraddy Holiday Park which is located some 3miles (5km) to the south of Aviemore on the south side of the B9152 between Aviemore and Kincraig. It is acceptable to use the car park beside the Alvie Forest Food kitchen and cafe, which is on the left as you enter the holiday park.

Walk back out to the entrance and turn left up the private estate road to Kinrara, soon crossing a bridge over the railway then the Speyside Way, which crosses the road. About 400m from the railway, turn off left onto a track which rises past trees and through a gate into a field. Continue on the grassy track to the top right edge of the field. There are fine views ahead to **Creag Dhubh** [18], the Argyll Stone torr visible on its summit crest, with Sgòran Dubh Mòr to its right then **Sgòr Gaoith** [21], then south over the Inshriach Forest and down Strathspey. Exit the field and follow the path uphill through beautiful pine, alder, birch and juniper woodland alive with sound of birdcalls. As the gradient eases, keep an eye out for a path on the right which leads to the Waterloo Cairn, partially hidden by trees, and reached by a short climb. The inscription on the plaque, erected by George Gordon (the 5th Duke of

START & FINISH: Dalraddy Holiday Park (NH858083)
DISTANCE: 5.75km; 3.5 miles
HEIGHT GAIN: 150m
APPROX TIME: 2hrs

Gordon and Marquis of Huntly) reads:

To the Memory of Sir Robert Macara of the 42nd Regiment or Royal Highlanders, Colonel John Cameron of the 92nd Regiment of Gordon Highlanders and their Brave Countrymen who gloriously fell at the Battle of Waterloo in June 1815. Erected by the most noble The Marquis of Huntly August 16th 1815.

Continue on the track crossing the narrowing between the highpoints where there is an open outlook to Cairn Gorm and an expansive view down the Spey Valley. Exposed rock here is a reminder that, like **Ord Bàn & Kennapole Hill** [19] opposite, this hill is a large scale example of roche moutonnee (see p43), created and left behind by the glacier that flowed down the valley during the ice age.

Shortly, the plinth and tall granite column of the Duke of Gordon's Monument comes into view. Standing on the highest point of Torr Alvie (358m) and at a height of 90 feet (27m), the pillar towers above the surrounding woodland and is a distinctive feature, visible from miles around. An 80 foot high memorial column to the Duke was also erected on Lady Hill near Elgin, that one featuring a statue of the Duke on its top.

Built in 1840, the inscription on the Torr Alvie column reads:

Erected in memory of His Grace George Fifth and last Duke of Gordon G.C.B, General in the British Army, Colonel of the Third Regiment of Foot Guards, Governor of the Castle of Edinburgh, Lord Lieutenant of Aberdeenshire &C &C &C, who died on the 28th of May 1836 in the sixty sixth year of his age. He was a generous landlord, a patriotic highlander and a brave soldier – at once the delight of the noble and the friend of the poor.

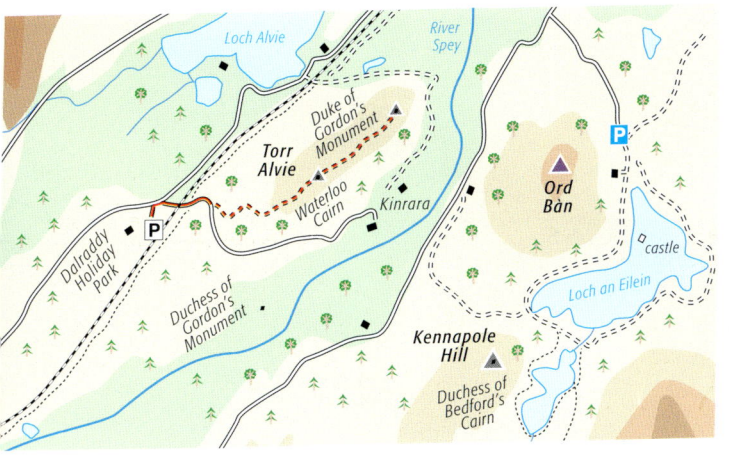

Torr Alvie

Waterloo Memorial

Torr Alvie lies in the grounds of Kinrara on the Alvie Estate, once a Gordon estate where much of the landscaping was overseen by George Gordon's mother, the Duchess of Gordon, who stayed in the summer house there. Her daughter, and George's sister, Lady Georgiana Gordon, became the Duchess of Bedford, to whom there is a memorial on Kennapole hill on the other side of the River Spey (see p123). Georgiana spent time living in Glen Feshie with her lover, the celebrated Victorian sculptor and artist Edwin Landseer (see p149).

From the far side of the monument there are views north up the Spey Valley over Aviemore. The summit area is the site of an ancient hillfort, although little of this now remains. Return the same way.

Torr Alvie

Duke of Gordon's Monument
Initially a Colonel in the 3rd Regiment of Foot Guards (now the Scots Guards), George Gordon (5th Duke of Gordon and Marquis of Huntly) was a professional soldier who rose to the rank of General. He commanded the 92nd (Gordon Highlanders) Regiment of Foot, originally raised by his father as the 100th Regiment of Foot to fight in the French Revolutionary Wars.

The regiment was recruited from Lochaber, Badenoch and Strathspey, and from Banff, Elgin and Aberdeen with the Highlanders coming into their own in the mountains of the Pyrenees where they took part in every action. During the Napoleonic Wars the regiment fought at the Battle of Waterloo where a famous incident took place when a cavalry charge by the Scots Greys saw some of the Gordon Highlanders hang onto the legs and stirrups of the cavalry in order to reach the enemy.

The regiment went on to see action in the Boer Wars in South Africa and in WWI on the Western Front where they suffered over 29,000 casualties, of whom some 9,000 died, which had huge impact on the Highland community.

In 1940, in the early days of WWII, the Gordon Highlanders were part of the ill-fated 51st Highland Division which was forced to surrender whilst attempting to evacuate at St Valery in the week following the Dunkirk evacuations. The former St Valery refuge above Stag Rocks on Cairn Gorm was named after this event. Duly reformed, the regiment took part in the D Day landings. In recent times they became the 1st Battalion The Highlanders (Gordon, Seaforth & Cameron), which is now The Highlanders, 4th Battalion The Royal Regiment of Scotland (4 Scots) with tours of duty in Iraq and Afghanistan.

The Gordon Highlanders regiment has over 120 battle honours and 19 Victoria Cross awards for valour.

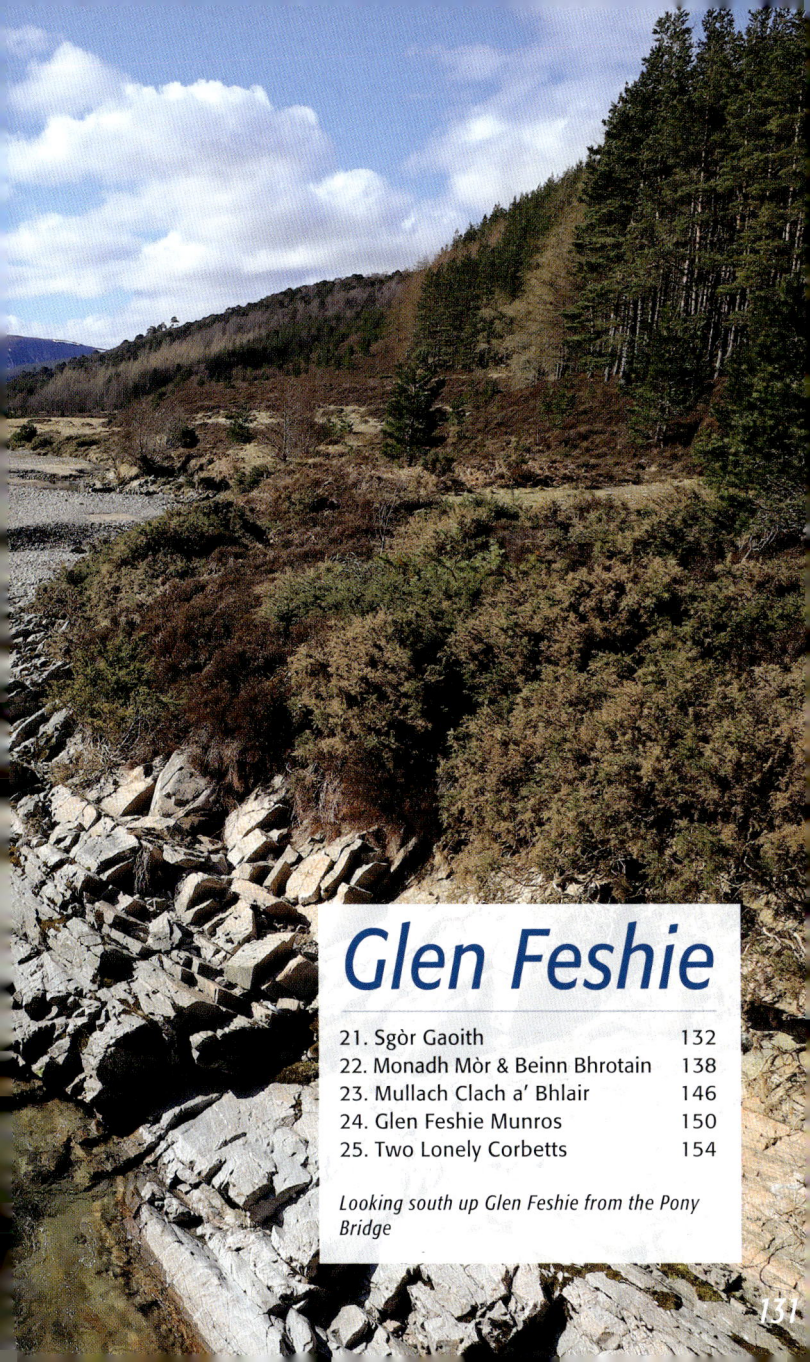

Glen Feshie

21. Sgòr Gaoith	132
22. Monadh Mòr & Beinn Bhrotain	138
23. Mullach Clach a' Bhlair	146
24. Glen Feshie Munros	150
25. Two Lonely Corbetts	154

Looking south up Glen Feshie from the Pony Bridge

Sgòr Gaoith
Windy Peak

Sgòr Gaoith and Loch Eanaich

Pronounced Skor Goo-ee, this Munro grants perhaps the finest view of all within the Cairngorms National Park. Its sharp summit clings to the edge of cliffs that plunge some 500m towards the steely waters of Loch Eanaich, with the scoured corries of Braeriach's huge western flanks rising beyond – it is simply breathtaking.

Sgòr Gaoith translates as Windy Peak and with its exposed summit sitting at the north-western edge of the Cairngorms it is certainly open to the elements. It forms the highpoint of the Invereshie and Inshriach National Nature Reserve, one of nine NNRs that lie within the Cairngorms National Park. The reserve covers an area of 3600 hectares where scatterings of rowan, birch, aspen, alder and juniper sit amongst large swathes of Caledonian and Scots pine. Other habitats within the reserve include blanket bog, montane grassland and alpine heath. As you would expect, the flora and fauna is incredibly diverse, with an abundance of mosses, lichens and fungi, as well as animals, birds and insects.

Lying between Speyside and Gleann Eanaich at the western edge of the main Cairngorm massif, Sgòr Gaoith together with its satellites occupies more ground than Braeriach, although it's not as high, or as bulky. It has five secondary Munro Tops (see p5), one of only three Munros to have as many. As well as climbing the main summit, this route takes in four of these Tops; the fifth being an outlier more easily included with the **Glen Feshie Munros** [24] route, which links Mullach Clach a' Bhlàir with Sgòr Gaoith.

The lower reaches of this circuit

START & FINISH: Allt Ruadh car park (NH853012)
DISTANCE: 17.5km; 11 miles
HEIGHT GAIN: 940m; 3080ft
APPROX TIME: 6–7hrs

follows excellent paths through, and back into, the Invereshie and Inshriach National Nature Reserve. However, much of the higher ground away from Sgòr Gaoith is generally pathless.

The ascent is made from a small car park in a clearing off a forest track, on the left side of the minor road that runs up the east side of the River Feshie, between Feshiebridge and Auchlean. This is just before the bridge across the Allt Ruadh, just over 1 mile (2km) beyond the entrance to the Cairngorm Gliding Club, whose gliders you may well see flying.

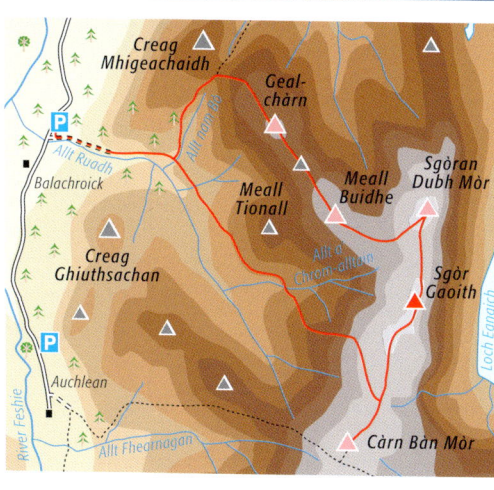

Leave the car park and take the grassy track that strikes east through woodland into the Invereshie and Inshriach NNR. After 650m the woodland thins, at which point bear left onto a path, rising steadily through gorgeous Caledonian

Creag Ghiuthsachan from the Allt Ruadh path

Sgòr Gaoith

pine woodland high above the Allt Ruadh. After the path levels off, go left at a fork and ascend north-east, with the woodland quickly replaced by open hillside. The route, which can be a little boggy, leads to a col separating Creag Mhigeachaidh and Geal-chàrn, where fine views open out across the reserve and Speyside.

Leave the path (which continues down the other side) for the rougher,

Geal-chàrn from Meall Buidhe

pathless lower slopes of Geal-chàrn. It is a steep climb, across spongy, heathery ground interspersed with short bouldery sections, and progress is slow, but the gradient relents when the broad summit ridge is reached at a cairn.

A short, gradual climb reaches Geal-chàrn's 920m summit (a Munro Top) and a fantastic view that takes in Glen Feshie, Ben Alder, Creag Meaghaidh and across the Spey Valley to the

> ### Glen Feshie
> *Regarded by many as the most beautiful glen in the Cairngorms National Park, Glen Feshie runs down the west side of the mountains forming the high Cairngorm Plateau. Its name means Sheltered Place from the Stormy Blasts, this sheltered nature being aided by its U-shaped topography, formed by glaciation. It is thought that humans began to exploit Glen Feshie about 2500 years ago, prompted to settle by great tracts of woodland, including Scots pine, rowan, alder, oak and birch, which provided materials for shelter and fuel.*
>
> *Red deer roaming the woodland would have yielded a key food source supplemented with plants and berries found within the woodland floor. Cattle would also have grazed in the woodland, as well as along the banks of the River Feshie, a rich source of fish for those who lived here. In the past, just like the Làirig Ghru and the Làirig an Laoigh, Glen Feshie was an important drove road allowing a natural through route for cattle to be driven from the Highlands to the markets in the south. It was also a route used by the likes of Queen Victoria who travelled through, the glen by pony on her way from, and back to, Balmoral in Deeside.*

Sgòr Gaoith

Monadh Liath. Closer at hand is Creag Dubh [18], with the Argyll Stone visible, and Càrn Eilrig [17] opposite. Cairn Gorm and the top of the Northern Corries are seen over Creag an Leth-choin, with Braeriach to the right, then the next four rounded summits in this circuit.

Continue southwards along a section of featureless ridge, dropping to a narrow col, which is crossed, to make a steady pull onto the rounded wind-scoured summit of Meall Buidhe (976m) another Munro Top; the low-cut moss and grass lending to its anglicised translation of Yellow Hill.

After another short descent, a steep rise east leads to a saddle on the main ridge linking Sgòran Dubh Mòr with Sgòr Gaoith to its south. A path runs along the ridge here and is followed north, gradually up onto the top of Sgòran Dubh Mòr (1111m), the third Munro Top of the route. The view of Gleann Eanaich and north-east along the frontal edge of the Cairngorm massif to Ben Rinnes is outstanding, with Braeriach and the deep bowls of Coire Bogha-cloiche, Coire nan Clach and Coire Dhondail particularly catching the eye.

Return to the saddle then make the easy climb to Sgòr Gaoith's pointed summit, with the final push hugging the lip of the sheer cliffs and buttresses that plunge almost vertically from the summit towards Loch Eanaich. The summit cairn is perched on the edge and again the view is staggering, dominated by the immense form of Braeriach on the other side of the deep Gleann Eanaich trough.

The path continues south-west, initially round the rim of Coire na Caillich then away from it to a broad col at 1012m where it peters out. Continue south-west with the ground rising onto Càrn Bàn Mòr (1052m), its

Sgòr Gaoith

Approaching Sgòr Gaoith from Càrn Bàn Mòr

broad, flat summit marked with a stone shelter. Here the vista extends across the wild and lonely plateau of the Mòine Mhòr (see p143) to **Monadh Mòr & Beinn Bhrotain** [22]. Visible through the gap between Cairn Toul and Monadh Mòr is Lochnagar, whilst to the south, in the corner of the high Cairngorm plateau, **Mullach Clach a' Bhlàir** [23] rises enough to give it Munro status.

Return to the col at 1012m, from where a steep descent north-west across the slope initially crosses rough

Raven
Jet-black in appearance, the raven is a splendid bird, and one conspicuous in the Cairngorms. Bigger than a buzzard and with a thick neck and powerful bill, the raven is wholly capable of defending its territory throughout the year. Nesting normally takes place on a cliff edge or overhanging crag, with food and water for their young being carried in a throat pouch. Highly intelligent, ravens have an uncanny way of detecting your presence and winging-in from afar, croaking to seemingly make you aware of them, or sitting on a highpoint awaiting your arrival. They are amazing fliers, often performing aerial acrobatics with other members of their family, seemingly just for your pleasure.

Sgòr Gaoith

Geal-chàrn from Meall Buidhe on the descent off Càrn Bàn Mòr

and at times stony ground onto the broad spur descending from Sgòr Gaoith. The incline quickly eases with the ground underfoot improving to reach the start of a good path at NN889986, which is followed down to the Allt a' Chrom-alltain.

Cross the burn and continue on the path, which traverses the lower slopes of Meall Tionall, keeping to the main path all the way down. After crossing the Allt a' Coire na Cloiche, enter Caledonian pine woodland again, soon descending across the Allt nam Bò to continue back to the start as for the outward route.

Allt Ruadh path – Inshriach National Nature Reserve

22 Monadh Mòr & Beinn Bhrotain
Across the Mòine Mhòr

Beinn Bhrotain from Monadh Mòr

Monadh Mòr and Beinn Bhrotain, both Munros, lie to the south-west and south of Cairn Toul and The Devil's Point, at the southern end of the Làirig Ghru, at the junction with Glen Geusachan, Glen Dee and Glen Luibeg. They are both quite big mountains, but they are linked by a high col at 975m, so are conveniently paired.

However, they are not so conveniently located, and routes to them are lengthy. They are generally ascended from Linn of Dee near Braemar, usually with the aid of a bike, but a slightly shorter on foot route can be made from Glen Feshie. This crosses the high upland plateau of the Mòine Mhòr (see p143) and unless some navigational challenge is required, it is a route best undertaken on a day when the tops are clear.

Start from a car park on the left, just after the minor road that runs up the east side of the River Feshie leaves the Invereshie and Inshriach National Nature Reserve (see p132) and enters the open. This is about 4 miles (6.75km) south of Feshiebridge and

START & FINISH: Auchlean Car Park (NN851985)
DISTANCE: 29km; 18 miles
HEIGHT GAIN: 1575m; 5165ft
APPROX TIME: 9hrs 30mins–10hrs 30mins

half a mile (1km) before the road ends at Auchlean.

Walk south along the road and before reaching its end at the estate cottage and outbuildings at Auchlean go left through a gate; there is a boulder with a sign for All Routes Please. Continue along a track then a path, past the Upper Glen Feshie route which is signed off right on a boulder, and go through a gate into the forest. The path makes a rising traverse through the woodland with fine views up Glen Feshie to Càrn Dearg Mòr, before swinging uphill to the left through gradually thinning out trees. Traditionally known as the Foxhunter's Path after a family of local hunters, it is now a well-engineered path that ascends the lower slopes of Càrn Bàn Mòr's north-west spur, high above the Allt Fhearnagan. After passing the side of a small col, the

Allt Fhearnagan path

path continues a little more steeply onto the shoulder at a small cairn just south of the summit.

Mullach Clach a' Bhlàir can be seen to the south and the route from there followed by Glen Feshie Munros [24] arrives here. Ahead lies the vast expanse of the Mòine Mhòr, bordered

Crossing the Mòine Mhòr past Loch nan Cnapan with Sgòr Gaoith beyond

Monadh Mòr & Beinn Bhrotain

by the slopes of Braeriach and Cairn Toul, and the sightly lower Monadh Mòr to the right. Follow the main route ahead, an atv track, downhill to the south-east across featureless terrain and onto a slight rise at 957m, passing a path off right (the route from or to, Mullach Clach a' Bhlàir). Follow the track eastwards, downhill to where it ends above the grassy-banked Allt Sgairnich at the head of a valley.

Drop to the burn and cross it, which can usually be done dry on stepping stones. Follow a path down the other side for 275m or so to a cairn and go left to reach an atv track crossing the shallow col at 876m above Loch na Cnapan. Continue on the track to make the short ascent onto the flat top of Tom Dubh (918m), passing first one cairn, then just below another that marks the top. Interestingly, this is a subsidiary Munro Top (see p5) of Monadh Mòr and one of the most esoteric and remote of all the Tops. The Cairngorms reindeer herd visits

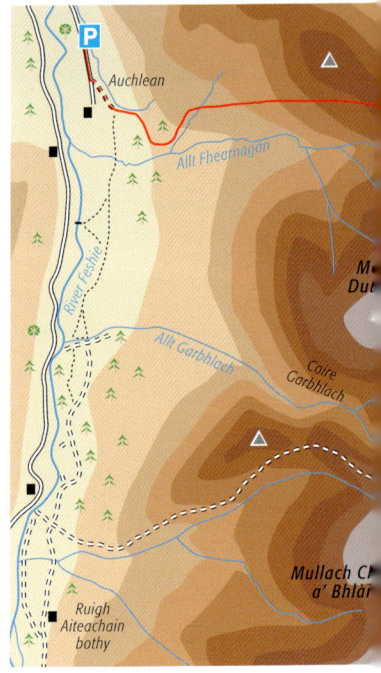

these parts, so keep an eye out.

Descend the atv track and a path slightly north of east into the shallow valley containing the Allt Luineag to just above where a burn feeds in on the far side at NN925953. Draining the surrounding slopes, the Allt Luineag is a fairly substantial river and one of the major headwaters that becomes the River Eidart. The crossing can be made on stepping stones, but there are times it may require a wade. If the water is running high, it could be awkward, or impassable.

Climb uphill to the side of the feeder burn, then ascend a grassy slope between the boulder fields onto the broad north ridge of Monadh Mòr and swing south to gain the summit cairn (1113m). To the east, steep slopes

Crossing the Allt Luineag

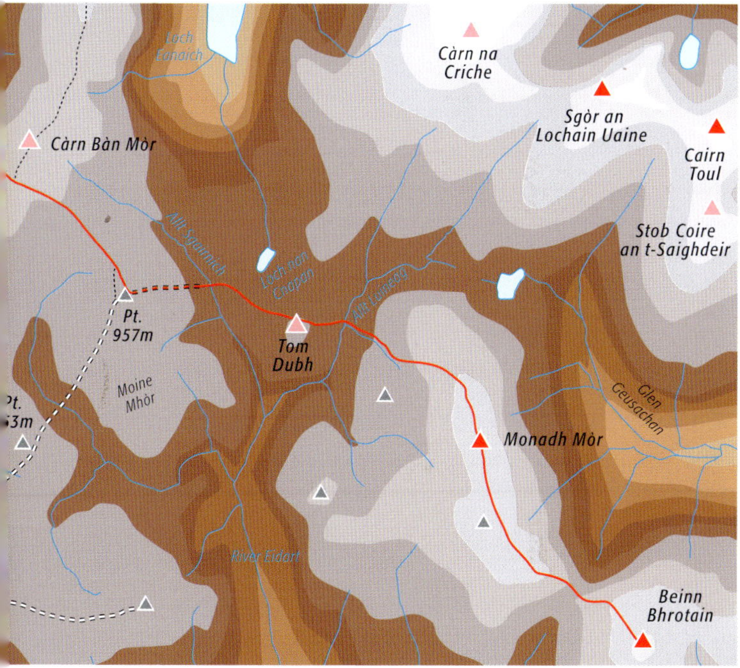

Monadh Mòr & Beinn Bhrotain

The Devil's Point with Ben Macdui and Derry Cairngorm beyond from the col

141

Monadh Mòr & Beinn Bhrotain

Monadh Mòr from Beinn Bhrotain

plunge into the impressive deep bowl of Glen Geusachan, formed between the steep flanks of Cairn Toul's Stob Coire an t-Saighdeir and The Devil's Point on the north side and on the south side by the equally steep-sided Beinn Bhrotain, which is now in view. To the east Ben Macdui shows its true stature with Beinn a' Bhuird beyond, then Mount Keen and Lochnagar. The view on the west side is far ranging; Ben Nevis and Creag Meaghaidh with its notched window are prominent.

Continue south along a path which runs below the ridge and the minor 1110m south top, then swing south-east over the Leac Ghorm (Green Cheek) where a cairn just off the path

Braeriach, Sgòr an Lochain Uaine, Cairn Toul and Ben Macdui right from Monadh Mòr

Monadh Mòr & Beinn Bhrotain

marks a fine viewpoint on the edge of the steep drop into Glen Geusachan. Descend the path quite steeply to the narrow col at 975m that separates the hills, then go up the other side to reach the extensive summit boulder field.

There is no defined route through this, but by climbing up and right, utilising the larger flatter rocks, the ascent is much easier than expected. On reaching the top, one of the wind-shelter cairns contains the trig pillar. At 1157m, the summit is higher than Monadh Mòr and being a bit further to the south and east, the views are that bit more extensive. The return to Auchlean, back the same way, is straightforward, but long!

Braeriach, Sgòr an Lochain Uaine and Cairn Toul across the Mòine Mhòr

Mòine Mhòr

This Great Moss or Peat Bog is the high plateau that lies between the tops forming the western edge of the Northern Cairngorms above Glen Feshie and the higher tops of Braeriach and Monadh Mòr to the east. To its north it drains into the Gleann Eanaich glacial trough and to the west into the deep bowl of Coire Gharblach. However the principal drainage from the Mòine Mhòr is south into the channel down which the River Eidart flows on its way to joining the River Feshie. In times of heavy rain or snow melt the volume of water is considerable. Unlike the neighbouring Braeriach and Ben Macdui plateaux, the Mòine Mhòr is much greener and softer, and sitting at an altitude of around 900m it is reckoned to be the largest expanse of high altitude blanket bog in the country. Some may deem it a featureless landscape, but it is an incredibly important habitat, with a low mattress of lichen, mosses, and other vegetation which provides rich nutrients for a vast array of insects and birds. Ongoing research is being carried out into the Mòine Mhòr, the climatic changes that have affected it, and what effects restoring the natural peatland might have in acting as a carbon sink, where more CO_2 is taken up through plant photosynthesis than is released through decay.

Braeriach from Sgòran Dubh Mòr - Coire Bogha-cloiche, Coire nan Clach and Coire Dhondail

23 Mullach Clach a' Bhlàir
The plateau's edge

Descending the south-west ridge of Mullach Clach a' Bhlàir towards Druim nam Bò

Sitting in the south-west corner of the Cairngorm plateau, the Munro of Mullach Clach a' Bhlàir is linked to its neighbours by the wild expanse of the Mòine Mhòr (see p143), the high moorland plateau that sits at an altitude of around 900m. Whilst it is an unremarkable summit in itself, the walk to it, and back from it, along Glen Feshie is very pleasant. It is also an outstanding viewpoint.

Start from a car park on the left, just after the minor road that runs up the east side of the River Feshie leaves the Invereshie and Inshriach National Nature Reserve and enters the open. This is about half a mile (1km) before the road ends at Auchlean and about 4 miles (6.75km) south of Feshiebridge.

Walk south down the road towards the estate cottage and outbuildings at Auchlean, then after 750m turn left through a gate at a boulder with a sign for All Routes Please. Follow the track for 300m then turn right along a path, signed to Upper Glen Feshie on another boulder. Keep to the flat floor of the glen and go through a gate to ford the Allt Fhearnagan; normally a simple crossing.

An excellent path continues across heather moorland for nearly 2km to reach the Allt Garbhlach. The banks have been washed-out here and although there is normally no problem with the crossing, it may require care at times, especially if the water is running high. A path leads to another crossing point upstream.

On the other side, a path leads into the forest, initially dominated by planted conifers, to reach a track. Turn right, then left onto another constructed path and follow this for 500m through conifer and older Scots pine to reach a track, which is followed for 400m to a junction. Turn left here (signposted to

START & FINISH: Auchlean Car Park (NN851985)
DISTANCE: 26.5km; 16.5 miles
HEIGHT GAIN: 920m; 3020ft
APPROX TIME: 7hrs 30mins–8hrs 30mins

summit of Mullach Clach a' Bhlàir (1019m).

The panorama however, is splendid. Pointed Sgòr Gaoith rises to the north, reached from here by Glen Feshie Munros [24], whilst Braeriach, Cairn Toul, Sgòr an Lochain Uaine then Monadh Mòr & Beinn Bhrotain [22] form a great barrier rising from the Mòine Mhòr to the north-east and east. To the south-east and south the Glenshee mountains and Beinn a' Ghlo rise, whilst in the south-west and west a good portion of the Central Highlands from Ben Lawers to the Nevis Range (50 miles distant) and Creag Meagaidh vie for attention. To the north-west are the Monadh Liath mountains. Closer at hand the Two Lonely Corbetts [25], Càrn Dearg Mòr and Leathad an

the Ruigh Aiteachain bothy) on the main track and continue through more conifers out into the open to reach a track crossroads.

Turn left and make the long ascent up the track above the Allt Coire Chaoil into Coire Caol, which leads to fine views over craggy Coire Garbhlach; it is worth diverting from the track for a better view into this corrie. Higher up, as the track curves towards the plateau, the views start to open out and the distant pointed summit of Sgòr Gaoith [21] can be seen to the north. When the track reaches the plateau and forks, swing right for about 750m then follow an atv track up the final rise to a small cairn on the otherwise featureless and unremarkable

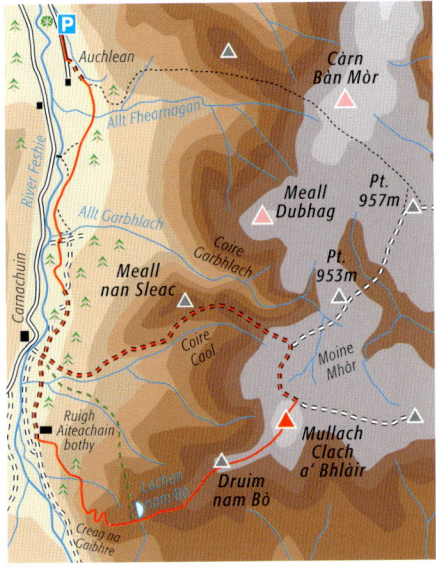

Mullach Clach a' Bhlàir

River Feshie
Rising beneath the top of Leathad an Taobhain (p154), the River Feshie drops north-east to where, rather than run east into the River Dee like the Geldie Burn some 200m away, it has taken that burn's headwaters and changed course westwards in a classic example of river capture. Soon joined by the River Eidart, which drains the Mòine Mhòr, it then curves around beneath Mullach Clach a' Bhlàir to flow north down Glen Feshie. From its source to where it joins the River Spey to the north-east of Kincraig it is some 35km in length. Glen Feshie and the River Feshie were formed by glaciers cutting their course through the landscape, leaving a classic example of a U-shaped valley with many associated glacial and post glacial landforms. Sedimentary sand and gravel terraces are evident, and date back 13,000 years to the melting glaciers. In places the river's floodplain is some 400m wide and it presents typical examples of braided channels where constantly changing mulitiple channels are formed in the deposition. It continues to be a highly active river and its power can be seen where its banks have been washed away in more recent times and by the large bridge at Carnachuin that was swept away in 2009.

Taobhain, can be seen.

Head south-west off the summit and follow an atv track down the mossy ridge out to Druim nam Bò. Drop to Lochan nam Bò and pass its south end. The atv track turns north here and can be followed all the way down to the track crossroads at the start of the climb up Coire Caol. However, this misses out on a visit to the Ruigh Aiteachain bothy and its lovely surroundings. Instead, leave the track and continue to a large cairn where the ridge ends above Creag na Gaibhre and steep slopes drop into Glen Feshie.

An overgrown stalkers' path, which is marked on maps, starts from the south side of the cairn, swings round the ridge, then descends north-west in zigzags to cross the burn by a stone bridge. The path continues down the

Lochan nam Bò and Carn Dearg Mòr (right)

Mullach Clach a' Bhlàir

edge above the burn to pass the first trees, then makes a long descending traverse across heathery ground before dropping to the track 100m from the estate renovated bothy at Ruigh Aiteachain. Some 700m beyond the bothy, rejoin the approach route at the foot of Coire Caol and follow this back.

> ### Edwin Landseer
> *Creator of the four lions below Nelson's Column in London, celebrated English artist Sir Edwin Landseer is perhaps better known for his Monarch of the Glen painting of a Scottish stag, the inspiration for which probably originated in Glen Feshie. Landseer spent much time in Scotland and in Glen Feshie where, despite being best known for his animal studies, he produced some fine landscapes, including a painting of the Loch Avon Basin similar to the photo on p38.*
> *Favoured in the Victorian age for his highland romanticism, he no doubt had a hand in increasing Scottish tourism in those times. In Glen Feshie, Landseer literally shacked-up with his lover, the Duchess of Bedford (see Kennapole Hill p122), in her turf-roofed wooden encampment close to the current bothy at Ruigh Aiteachain.*

24 Glen Feshie Munros
A high level traverse above Glen Feshie

Across Coire Garbhlach to Meall Dubhag, left, pointed Sgòr Gaoith, centre, and distant Braeriach, Sgòr an Lochain Uaine and Cairn Toul

Following the western edge of the Northern Cairngorm plateau, this fine route links the two Munros above Glen Feshie and includes all five subsidiary Munro Tops (see p5) in the range. Good paths and tracks lead to and from the plateau from Glen Feshie making this a fairly straightforward, though long route. However, it should not be underestimated, especially in adverse conditions. The initial part of the route is the same as for the ascent of **Mullach Clach a' Bhlàir** [23].

Start from a car park on the left, just after the minor road that runs up the east side of the River Feshie leaves the Inveruishie and Inshriach National Nature Reserve (see p132) and enters the open. This is about half a mile (1km) before the road ends at Auchlean and about 4 miles (6.75km) south of Feshiebridge.

Walk south down the road towards the estate cottage and outbuildings at Auchlean, which are hidden in a dip, then after 750m turn left through a gate at a boulder with a sign for All Routes Please. Follow the track for 300m then turn right along a path, signed to Upper Glen Feshie on another boulder. Keep to the flat floor of the glen and go through a gate to cross the Allt Fhearnagan. Fording this is usually straightforward.

An excellent path continues across heather moorland for nearly 2km to reach the Allt Garbhlach. The banks have been washed-out here and although there is normally no problem with the crossing, it may require care at times, especially if the water is running high. A path leads to another crossing point upstream.

On the other side, a path leads into

START & FINISH: Auchlean Car Park (NN851985)
DISTANCE: 34km; 21 miles
HEIGHT GAIN: 1240m; 4070ft
APPROX TIME: 9–10hrs Leaving a bike at the northern car park for the return along the road, would save about 25mins

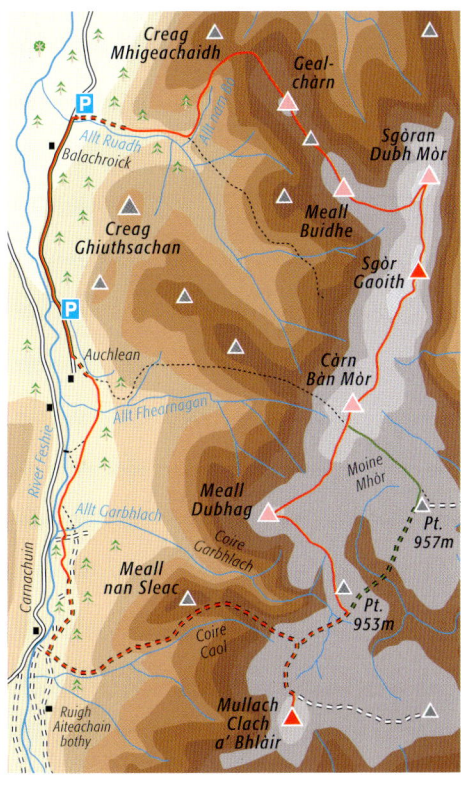

the forest, initially dominated by planted conifers, to reach a track. Turn right, then left onto another constructed path and follow this for 500m through conifer and older Scots pine to reach a track, which is followed for 400m to a junction. Turn left here on the main track (signposted to the Ruigh Aiteachain bothy) and continue through more conifers out into the open to reach a track crossroads.

Turn left and make the long ascent up the track above the Allt Coire Chaoil, into Coire Caol, which leads to fine views over craggy Coire Garbhlach; it is worth diverting from the track for the view into this corrie. Higher up, as the track curves around towards the plateau and the summit of Mullach Clach a' Bhlàir, the distant pointed summit of Sgòr Gaoith comes into view to the north. When the track reaches the plateau and forks, swing right for about 750m then follow an atv track up the final rise to a small cairn on the flat summit of Mullach Clach a' Bhlàir (1019m).

The summit views are wide and far-ranging. Across the Mòine Mhòr, to the north and east, the western peaks of the Cairngorms form a great barrier, whilst in an arc from Lochnagar to the south-east, the panorama stretches across the Glen Shee and Perthshire hills to the Central Highlands and Creag Meagaidh with its distinctive notched window.

Return to the track junction at the top of Coire Caol, then turn right and follow the track that heads north-east towards pointed Sgòr Gaoith. This track undulates across the Mòine Mhòr (see p143) over Pt.953m and Pt.957m to end after 4km above the Allt Sgairnich. It provides the simplest means

Glen Feshie Munros

Mullach Clach a' Bhlàir's summit, pointed Sgòr Gaoith, left, and distant Braeriach, Sgòr an Lochain Uaine and Cairn Toul, right

(especially in poor conditions) of gaining Càrn Bàn Mòr, leaving it after 3.25km on flat-topped Pt.957m to follow a link path north to an atv track. This track is followed north-west across the featureless watershed then up to a small cairn on the shoulder of Càrn Bàn Mòr on the edge of the Mòine Mhòr.

However, in good conditions it is quicker and more scenic to gain this point by leaving the track 1.25km along it on Pt.953m, after crossing the first two burns at the head of Coire Garbhlach. Head north-west across the other burn flowing into this corrie, then follow the edge to reach Meall Dubhag. It is a superb vantage point from which to gaze down into Fionnar Choire and Coire Garbhlach, as well as to the upper reaches of Glen Feshie where the **Two Lonely Corbetts [25]**, Càrn Dearg Mòr & Leathad an Taobhain, can be picked out. Grassy slopes then lead north-east to a col, from where a faint path is followed northward to the small cairn on the shoulder of Càrn Bàn Mòr.

This marks the highpoint of the path to **Monadh Mòr & Beinn Bhrotain [22]**, which ascends from Glen Feshie above the Allt Fhearnagan before it drops to the Mòine Mhòr to join the track on Pt.957m.

Ascend north on another path, which disappears on rocky ground, to gain the summit of Càrn Bàn Mòr with its shelter cairn. Although the top is nondescript the view is anything but. Ben Alder, Ben Nevis, Creag Meagaidh with its distinctive notched window, and their neighbouring hills form a dramatic backdrop to the west, whilst the massive bulk of Braeriach and flat-topped Cairn Toul rise spectacularly to the east. **Sgòr Gaoith [21]**, which Càrn Bàn Mòr is a secondary Munro Top of, rises to the north, whilst to the south-east Monadh Mòr and Beinn Bhrotain define the edge of the Mòine Mhòr.

Descend north-east to a wide col, picking up a path again, and continue up the broad, grassy slope ahead before traversing the rim of Coire na Caillich towards pointed Sgòr Gaoith. It is a spectacular summit with the cairn perched on the edge of the rocky buttresses that plunge steeply east to Loch Eanaich. The view over the loch and the impressive trough of Gleann Eanaich is dominated by Braeriach and the glaciated bowls of Coire

Glen Feshie Munros

Bogha-cloiche, Coire nan Clach and Coire Dhondail.

Sgòran Dubh Mòr

Leave the summit and descend the path easily north, overlooking Gleann Eanaich, to a saddle then continue to the top of Sgòran Dubh Mòr (1111m), another Munro Top. Return towards the saddle and descend west, passing over a knoll, then onto the rounded summit of Meall Buidhe (976m), another Munro Top.

Continue northwards over another knoll on a section of featureless ridge, then ascend to the summit cairn of Geal-chàrn (920m), the fifth Munro Top and final summit on the route. Take in the view, then follow the rough and pathless ridge in a north-westerly direction, descending through bouldery ground to gain a path that crosses the col separating Geal-chàrn from Creag Mhigeachaidh to the north-west.

Turn left here and follow the path south-west, downhill towards Glen Feshie. The going is a bit boggy in places as open hillside gives way to woodland, but a better path traversing above the Allt Ruadh is soon reached. Turn right onto this and follow it down into the glen, through beautiful Caledonian pine forest to reach a track.

Go right and follow the grassy track through the Invereshie and Inshriach National Nature Reserve to reach a small car park before the main road through the glen. Turn left and follow the road for 3km back to the Auchlean car park. If a bike has been left here on the way past in the morning, this will enable a swift return.

Sgòran Dubh Mòr, right, and distant Cairn Gorm and Braeriach from Geal-chàrn

25 Two Lonely Corbetts
Leathad an Taobhain and Càrn Dearg Mòr

The view from Leathad an Taobhain. The pointed summit of Sgòr Gaoith, is to the left, with Braeriach, Sgòr an Lochain Uaine, Cairn Toul, Monadh Mòr and Beinn Bhrotain to the right

Leathad an Taobhain and Càrn Dearg Mòr rise within a vast tract of featureless ground on the fringe of the main Northern Cairngorm massif, between Glen Feshie, Glen Tromie and the Forest of Atholl. The approach from the north has the benefit of travelling through beautiful Glen Feshie, as well as having good tracks that run almost all the way onto both summits.

Despite this, and the fact that they are both Corbetts, these hills are infrequently climbed and they have an air of remoteness. This is especially true of Leathad an Taobhain, which is surrounded by a host of other inconspicuous rolling hills, its summit poking up enough to be the highest point for some distance.

The route begins from a car park on the left, just after the minor road that runs up the east side of the River Feshie leaves the Invereshie and Inshriach National Nature Reserve (see p132) and enters the open. This is about half a mile (1km) before the road ends at Auchlean and about 4 miles (6.75km) south of Feshiebridge.

Walk south down the road towards the estate cottage and outbuildings at Auchlean, then after 750m turn left through a gate at a boulder with a sign for All Routes Please. Follow the track

START & FINISH: Auchlean Car Park (NN851985)
DISTANCE: 34.5km (21.5 miles)
HEIGHT GAIN: 1085m; 3560ft
APPROX TIME: 9hrs 30mins–10hrs 30mins

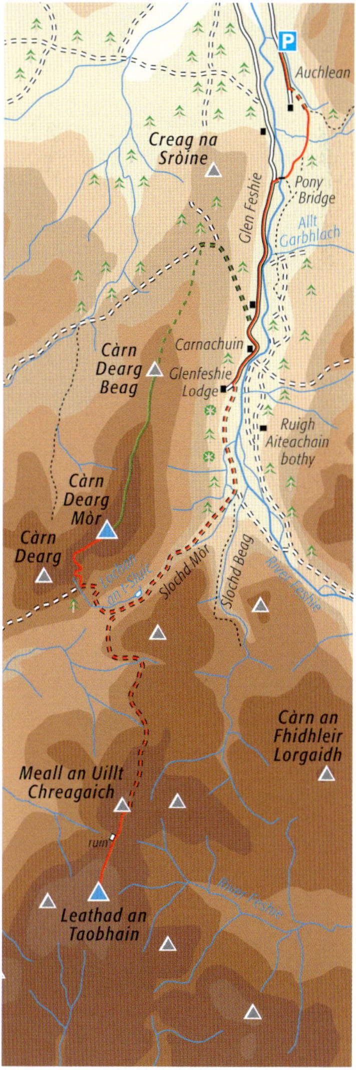

for 300m then turn right along a path, signed to Upper Glen Feshie on another boulder. Keep to the flat floor of the glen and go through a gate to cross the Allt Fhearnagan; normally easy but it could be awkward when the water is high.

Continue along the well-constructed path for 450m, then turn right to follow another path to the River Feshie, which is crossed via a wooden bridge known as the Pony Bridge. Once over, take a stepped path on the right to a track and follow this to a surfaced estate road just above, then go left.

The road runs south through a

Two Lonely Corbetts

stunning section of Glen Feshie, where the hillsides are cloaked in Scots pine, birch and juniper. Birds such as crossbill and crested tit may well be spotted. It is a lovely walk along the glen and there is a good view into the deep and narrow Coire Garbhlach on the other side, which separates Sgòr Gaoith [21] and its satellite tops from Mullach Clach a' Bhlàir [23].

After 2.5km, a track on the right is passed (used on the return journey by the north ridge alternative descent) then a number of attractive cottages at Carnachuin. In a further 500m or so, where the road heads to Glenfeshie Lodge on the right, go left onto a rough track that travels above the wide floodplain of the River Feshie with fine views across to Mullach Clach a' Bhlàir and its grassy west facing corries. The landscape now begins to open out, highlighting the beautiful scenery the glen is renowned for.

Two Lonely Corbetts

The Pony Bridge, Carn Bàn Mòr, left, and Coire Garbhlach, right

After 2km the track splits again, at the ruin of the Ruigh-fionntaig shooting lodge, in front of the deep bowl of the Slochd Beag. Head right here (south-west), away from the river which curves round to the left.

An alternative approach to this point can be made by an easy bike ride of some 9km, from a parking area at NN842994 at the end of the public road along the west side of the glen. Those with the leg power might consider pedalling further, even to the end of the track, although it is an ascent of 450m!

From Ruigh-fionntaig, the route makes a steady climb through the narrow defile of the Slochd Mòr, offering a superb view back of Glen Feshie and Meall Dubhag over the top of Coire Garbhlach, with Mullach Clach a' Bhlàir to the right. Once past the solitary Lochan an t-Sluic the track climbs to a fork. Take the left branch and make a

Two Lonely Corbetts

Leathad an Taobhain from Meall an Uillt Chreagaich

gradual ascent up the side of the hill, enjoying the view as it opens out; across to the Munro Meall Cuaich near Drumochter, down into Glen Tromie and beyond to the Monadh Liath.

Higher, after swinging right across a burn, the track climbs more steeply onto the crest of Meall an Uillt Chreagaich (847m), passing just left of a small summit cairn, where it continues as an atv track. The view extends across a remote landscape with few signs of human habitation. The twin tops of Leathad an Taobhain now lie ahead; maps currently place the hill name against the lower west top, not the higher east top

A small cairn to the left of the track indicates a rough path that begins to drop into a lonely glen. Almost immediately it splits, so keep right and descend steeply (it can be boggy) to a small ruin at the right side of the col on the watershed between the headwaters of the River Tromie to the west and the source of the River Feshie to the east.

Once across a short section of flat, boggy ground a clearer path rises steadily south for the 150m ascent to the summit of Leathad an Taobhain. As

> ### Càrn Dearg Mòr – north ridge descent
> A worthwhile option is to stay high and go down the 5km-long ridge that extends northwards. The atv track drops gradually down this wide ridge with good views of Speyside and Glen Feshie, passing to the left of a trig pillar on Càrn Dearg Beag (694m) after 2.75km. The outlook, towards the high, rolling plateau above Glen Feshie, from Sgòr Gaoith and its Tops to Mullach Clach a' Bhlàir, is fantastic. This is actually 1km shorter than the return via the Slochd Mòr.
> Eventually the track disappears, after which rougher ground is crossed north-east to gain a track. Turn right down this to reach the road just north of Carnachuin and follow it back to the bridge over the River Feshie then return to Auchlean.

Two Lonely Corbetts

the rounded top is neared, the path skirts a little east of the summit and the last few metres to the lonely trig pillar are across grassy slopes.

At 912m Leathad an Taobhain is only 2.4m short of Munro status and were it that fraction higher it would rise above the magical 3000ft line and undoubtedly be more popular. However, the lack of traffic together with its elevated position amongst the rolling hills that surround it, give it a great sense of space and solitude to go with the expansive views; the high plateau of the Northern Cairngorms to the north-east being particularly captivating.

Retrace your steps all the way back to the fork above the Slochd Mòr, then go left onto a track that zigzags its way steeply up towards the saddle between Càrn Dearg and Càrn Dearg Mòr. Follow the track as it swings left to traverse the hillside then leave it for the atv track which climbs to the saddle, reached by a right fork. Continue north-east up the rounded ridge on the atv track to gain the

Descending towards Càrn Dearg Mòr

summit cairn on the flat top of Càrn Dearg Mòr (857m). The simplest return is back the same way via the Slochd Mòr and Glen Feshie; especially if a bike has been used.

mica *guides*
www.micapublishing.com

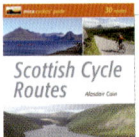
30 cycles
Scottish Cycle Routes
Volume 1
by Alasdair Cain

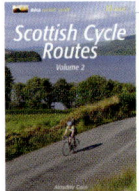
30 cycles
Scottish Cycle Routes
Volume 2
by Alasdair Cain

60 walks
The Pentland Hills
by Rab Anderson

60 walks
Lothian & Berwickshire Coast
by Keith Fergus

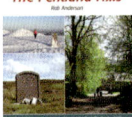
60 walks
Loch Lomond and The Trossachs National Park
Vol 1 – West
by Tom Prentice

60 walks
Loch Lomond and The Trossachs National Park Vol 2 – East
by Tom Prentice

60 walks
The Lakeland Fells
by Bernard Newman

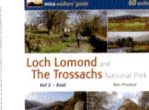
Chasing the Ephemeral
50 Routes for a Successful Scottish Winter
by Simon Richardson

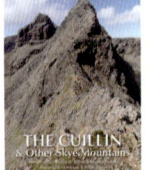
The Cuillin & Other Skye Mountains
The Cuillin Ridge & 100 select routes for mountain climbers & hillwalkers
by Tom Prentice

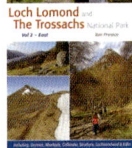

Cuillin Ridge Topo Guide
A photographic topo guide to the Cuillin Ridge
by Tom Prentice